SURVIVAL SPANISH
FOR
EMERGENCY RESPONDERS

FOR WHEN IT'S GOT TO BE DONE——AND YOU'RE IT

by

James Serrato

Edited by: Sandra Serrato

DISCLAIMER:

Please note that the author/publisher of this book is not responsible in any manner whatsoever for any mishap that may occur during the utilization of the information contained herein.

It is essential that before applying this material to any real-world situations, the reader become familiar with it—as thoroughly as possible. It is also strongly recommended that the reader, for his own benefit, keep this book near him for reference, until attaining mastery over the material.

STREE**T**WISE
TECHNOLOGIES

14080 Nacogdoches #302, San Antonio, Tx 78247
(210) 646-6290

Printed in San Antonio, Texas, USA
Second Printing
ISBN: 0-9635324-0-5
Library of Congress No.: 93-135292

ACKNOWLEDGEMENTS:

A work like this cannot be accomplished without the help of family and friends. My wife Sandra, for all the help and all the midnight oil we burned. My parents, Abelino (deceased) and Aurelia Serrato, and Frank and Lydia Martinez for enriching my life with not one, but two cultures. Albert and Celia Bache, along with Enrique Sanchez and Carlos Sanchez, and my brothers Ramon (deceased) and Abelino Serrato Jr., and my parents-in-law Paul and Vicki Casarez, for all their technical assistance. Barry and Kathy Dickinson, for all their help behind the computer. There are also several individuals without whom this list would not be complete: San Antonio Chief of Police William O. Gibson, Executive Officer Captain Richard Gleinser, Director of Training Captain Amadeo Ortiz. In-service Training Coordinator Sergeant Lawrence Keys, Cadet Training Coordinator Sergeant Jeffry Van Slycke, CLEAT Secretary/Treasurer Sergeant Harold Flammia, and Detective Jerry Clancy, President of the San Antonio Police Officer's Association. Bexar County Sheriff Ralph Lopez, Chief of Patrol Clyde Ross, Director of Staff Development Ms. Sandra Dworaczyk, Training Coordinator Lieutenant James Cantilli, and Training Supervisor Sergeant John Hubbard, AACOG Academy Director Mr. Ian "Buddy" Lovestock, TCLEOSE Executive Director Mr. Fred Toler, Program Administrator III Mr. Gerald Keown, and Program Administrator II Mr. George Hardin. Houston Police Department Training Instructor Officer Roman Chavez, Mr. Lawrence J. Souza, Attorney-at-law, Counsel for the San Antonio Police Officer's Association. Mr. and Mrs. Jim Burke and Miss Jennifer Burke, of Burke Publishing. My brothers/sisters of the San Antonio Police Department, for all their suggestions, and anyone that I may have inadvertantly failed to mention — I give you my heartfelt thanks and appreciation.

CONTENTS

James Serrato is a 27-year-old native of San Antonio, Texas. A husband, a father, and a Shorin-ryu karate-do martial artist. Officer Serrato joined the San Antonio Police Department in 1988, and elected to take the busy Westside as his duty assignment upon graduating the academy. Born and raised on the predominantly Hispanic Westside of the city, Officer Serrato felt proud to return to the community in which he grew up.

Officer Serrato attended Texas A & M University, upon completing high school, under full academic scholarship. He ceded his scholarship in order to return to his hometown and assume several family responsibilities. While attending Texas A & M University, he was awarded 14 hours (5 semesters) credit of college level Spanish, by challenge exam alone. Officer Serrato then went on to graduate from Wayland Baptist University. Aside from his patrol duties, he is a T.C.L.E.O.S.E. (Texas Commission on Law Enforcement Officers Standards and Education) certified police instructor and teaches "Survival Spanish" / Cultural Sensitivity and Awareness for the San Antonio Police Department, the Bexar County Sheriff's Department, A.A.C.O.G. (Alamo Area Council of Governments) and has also taught for the Houston Police Academy. To complement this manual, he has developed eight-hour, twenty-four hour and forty-hour schools, which are the absolute cutting edge on "Survival Spanish" and Cultural Awareness / Sensitivity training. The forty hour "Survival Spanish" / Cultural Sensitivity and Awareness school has been held, by invitation, at the Austin, Texas Headquarters of T.C.L.E.O.S.E.

Officer Serrato feels that the plight of the modern police officer is akin to that of the Viet Nam soldier. The sons and daughters of America that answered the call to duty then and there, like those

7

here and now, suffered to get the readily available technology—and even when they did, the "powers that be" kept the rules so that winning was, in reality, not an option. He hopes that one day soon, America will rally behind the war on crime and those who fight the war daily, as it did during Operation Desert Storm. This book is the maiden effort of Officer Serrato's newly-born company, STREETWISE TECHNOLOGIES, to produce useful and effective tools for law enforcement, as well as other emergency responders.

INTRODUCTION:

What you have before you, I have designed to be useful to the emergency responder that might come across a situation where Spanish is the only language spoken. I call this type of language barrier the "Deadly Disadvantage." It greatly increases the danger potential to the officer and those in his custody.

While still going through the San Antonio Police Academy, I realized that in many of the southern states—in fact throughout the United States—as police officers we are certain to come across many situations where Spanish will be the only language spoken. Worse yet, it might be the language spoken to purposefully keep you at such a definite disadvantage. Never underestimate the "Deadly Disadvantage," it can cost you your case ... or maybe even your life. Our chosen profession calls upon us to deal with potentially violent and extremely stressful situations, many of which will appear to come out of nowhere or snowball suddenly from a minor thing in but a few seconds. You may not have the time to get cover, much less an interpreter, or there may not be one available at all. Therefore, I suggest that you keep this easy-reference guide on your person while on duty or at least in your briefcase, where you can get to it.

My work reflects what I have found to be the more widely used terms of slang, Tex-mex, and proper Spanish. It is based on my personal experiences, both as and prior to becoming a policeman. This book, which began as a few simple lists for friends of mine, will give you a functional vocabulary—if you devote some coffee time and a little effort to it. We each work with the skills and tools that we acquire through our experiences and learning. You now have a very strong tool to fight against one of the many disadvantages the modern emergency responder faces.

9

I sincerely feel that this book will prove to be a great asset to any police department and/or officer that works in an environment with a Hispanic element. If fully utilized, this book can give you the edge. However, please bear in mind that it is not meant to create Spanish experts overnight. It will, though, serve you well by allowing you to be fully functional and effective during those times when it's got to be done—and you're it.

Always Good Luck,

James Serrato

CHAPTER 1

Summary of Principles

SOME ADVICE

As a professional, working in today's fast paced world, you can expect society to be critical of your every action. The media can work against us, or it can work for us. We cannot ever forget that their motivation (among others) is to become and remain a profitable enterprise. Their marketable product is information and they, like the public in general, work with the observable facts. Therefore, I suggest that we strive to practice our profession with the greatest sense of preciseness that we can muster. Stereotypes and misconceptions have been, and probably always will be, among our greatest pitfalls. If we are to effect change in them, it will have to come through the efforts of the individual and on a one-at-a-time basis.

Behavioral studies have shown that a lack of understanding any culture tends to enhance the retention of stereotypes. A strong criticism of the Hispanic culture(s), as a whole, is that they are pessimistic. Often the individual member is misrepresented as down-trodden, low-spirited, unhappy, or only content at best. This is an incorrect stereotype. We must take into consideration that, like many other cultures found in our United States, you can pretty much see a line of change in what is academically termed the 1st, 2nd and 3rd generations. The earlier/older the generation, the more likely it is that it will hold onto the traditionalist views of the culture. Be assured, the Hispanic is as much a vibrant, progressive, and resilient an individual as will be found in any culture.

It is also important to be aware that each locale of culture will be individualized to the area. By this I mean, it will share the major characteristics of the parent group, but it will also assimilate those of the dominant culture in the area; school children being a prime example of this. No one can become totally familiar with all of a culture, unless he becomes a full member of it. However, it is advisable that you become familiar with the language, norms, and practices of your community. It can and will make the difference for you.

ALPHABET:

A (AH)	B (BEH)	C (SEH)	D (DEH)
E (EH)	F (EH-FEH)	G (HEH)	H (AH-CHEH)
I (E)	J (HOH-TAH)	K (KAH)	L (EH-LEH)
LL (EH-YEH)	M (EH-MEH)	N (EH-NEH)	Ñ (EH-NYEH)
O (OH)	P (PEH)	Q (KOOH)	R (EH-RREH)
S (EH-SEH)	T (TEH)	U (OOH)	V (VEH)
W (DOH-BLEH-OOH)	X (EH-KIHS)	Y (E-GRIH-YEH-GAH)	Z (SEH-TAH)

NOTE: Some schools teach ch (CHEH) and rr (EH-RREH) as letters, with k and w being attributed to words of foreign origin.

VOWELS (PHONETICALLY):

A sounds like English Oscar
E sounds like English emerald
I sounds like English igloo
O sounds like English organ
U sounds like English zoo
Y sounds like English igloo or yam

Rules for Pronunciation:

1. Phonetic sounds are shorter in Spanish.

   <u>Example</u>: English no sounds like know
   Spanish no sounds like noh of north

2. C sounds like English K or S.

   <u>Example</u>: Head is cabeza (KAH-BEH-SAH)
   Fence is cerca (SEHR-KAH)

3. H is usually silent if it is the first letter in a word.

   <u>Example</u>: Speak is hablar (AH-BLAHR)

4. In Spanish, J and sometimes G sound like an English H.

   <u>Example</u>: Cage is   jaula (HOW-LAH)
   People is gente (HEHN-TEH)

5. LL sounds like an English Y.

   <u>Example</u>: Cry is llorar (YOH-RAHR)

6. Ñ makes the nyeh sound.

   <u>Example</u>: Treviño (TREH-VIH-NYOH)

7. R, when doubled, makes a rolled rrr sound, like when children imitate automatic fire.

   <u>Example</u>: Rice is arroz (AH-RROHS)

8. Z sounds like an English S.

    <u>Example</u>:   Shoe is zapato (SAH-PAH-TOH)

9. Ending in O mostly applies to the masculine form.

    <u>Example</u>:   Male dog is perro (PEH-RROH)

10. Ending in A mostly applies to the feminine form.

    <u>Example</u>:   Female dog is perra (PEH-RRAH)

11. Ending in ito/ita emphasizes little or cute.

    <u>Example</u>:   Little dog is perrito (PEH-RRIH-TOH)
             or   perrita (PEH-RRIH-TAH)

12. My use of H, as in NOH (see example #1), indicates shortening of the vowel sound.

13. My use of Y, as in lion (LEH-YOHN, see pg 28), indicates a flowing of sound between syllables.

We all work with the tools that we acquire through learning and experience. As human beings, it is our nature to develop our strengths so that they can compensate for our weaknesses. However, as a group, we have become almost intuitive in our actions. The so-called "sixth sense" is a formidable tool, so too the book you now hold. When using this tool, please keep in mind that, as with English, many words in Spanish can have dual meanings or unrecognized connotations. So keep the conversations as simple as possible and to the point. Here are a few other general rules to keep in mind:

1. Always remain aware that a few brief, not-understood words could blow your case ... or worse yet, cost you your life.

2. Use the index portion of this book for quick reference of unknown Spanish words you come across.

3. Your tone of voice, general demeanor, and body language will make this work for you —— or against you. Technique and approach are the key.

4. Remain aware of available translators; children are a very good resource, as are neighbors and/or onlookers. However, take into consideration their view of what has transpired; it may not be wise to involve them or they may be fearful to get involved. If and when you do use anyone to translate, be sure to get good identification on them. You may need it for a subpoena later.

5. When in doubt, get a Spanish speaker to cover you or at least switch over to an open channel for you to consult. It may even be possible for him to translate between you and your subject(s) right over the radio.

CHAPTER 2

Terminology

— ANATOMY

English	Spanish	Pronounced
ankle	tobillo	(TOH-BIH-YOH)
appendix	apendice	(AH-PEHN-DIH-SEH)
armpit [slang]	sobaco [arcas]	(SOH-BAH-KOH) [AHR-KAHS]
arms	brazos	(BRAH-SOHS)
back	espalda	(EHS-PAHL-DAH)
bald [slang]	calvo [pelon]	(KAHL-VOH) [PEH-LOHN]
beard	barba	(BAHR-BAH)
bladder	vejiga	(VEH-HIH-GAH)
body	cuerpo	(KOOH-WEHR-POH)
brain	ceso	(SEH-SOH)
bust	busto	(BOOHS-TOH)
chest	pecho	(PEH-CHOH)
crotch/groin [slang]	ingle [verijas]	(IHN-GLEH) [VEH-RIH-HAHS]
ears [slang]	oidos [orejas]	(OH-YIH-DOHS) [OH-REH-HAHS]
esophagus	esofago	(EH-SOH-FAH-GOH)

CHAPTER 2

ANATOMY ——

English	Spanish	Pronounced
eyes	ojos	(OH-HOHS)
face	cara	(KAH-RAH)
feet [slang]	pies [patas]	(PIH-YEHS) [PAH-TAHS]
fingers	dedos	(DEH-DOHS)
gall bladder	vesicula biliar	(VEH-SIH-KYUH-LAH) (BIH-LIH-YAHR)
hair	pelo / cabello	(PEH-LOH) / (KAH-BEH-YOH)
hands [slang]	manos [visa]	(MAH-NOHS) [VY-SAH]
head	cabeza	(KAH-BEH-SAH)
heart	corazon	(KOH-RAH-SOHN)
hips	caderas	(KAH-DEH-RAHS)
kidney	riñon	(RIH-NYOHN)
knee	rodilla	(ROH-DIH-YAH)
large intestine	intestino grueso	(IHN-TEHS-TIH-NOH) (GROOH-WEH-SOH)
legs	piernas	(PIH-YEHR-NAHS)

Terminology

— Anatomy

English	Spanish	Pronounced
liver	higado	(IH-GAH-DOH)
lungs	pulmones	(POOHL-MOH-NEHS)
mouth	boca	(BOH-KAH)
mustache	bigote	(BIH-GOH-TEH)
nails	uñas	(OOH-NYAHS)
neck	cuello / pescueso	(KWEH-YOH) / (PEHS-KWEH-SOH)
nose	nariz	(NAH-RIHS)
pancreas	pancreas	(PAHN-KREH-YAHS)
saliva	saliva	(SAH-LIH-VAH)
scar	cicatriz	(SIH-KAH-TRIHS)
small intestine	intestino delgado	(IHN-TEHS-TIH-NOH) (DEHL-GAH-DOH)
spit	escupo	(EHS-KOOH-POH)
spleen	bazo	(BAH-SOH)
stomach [slang]	estomago [pansa]	(EHS-TOH-MAH-GOH) [PAHN-SAH]
teeth	dientes	(DIH-YEHN-TEHS)

ANATOMY ——

English	Spanish	Pronounced
thumb	pulgar	(POOHL-GAHR)
thyroid gland	glandula tiroides	(GLAHN-DOOH-LAH) (TIH-ROH-IH-DEHS)
tongue	lengua	(LEHN-GWAH)
tracheal artery	traque arteria	(TRAH-KEH) (AHR-TEH-RIH-YAH)
waist	cintura	(SIHN-TOOH-RAH)

Terminology

— ANATOMY (SEX ORGANS)

English	Spanish	Pronounced
areola / nipple	peson	(PEH-SOHN)
anus	ano / fondillo	(AH-NOH) / (FOHN-DIH-YOH)
breasts [slang]	cenos [chiches] / [tetas]	(SEH-NOHS) [CHIH-CHES] / [TEH-TAHS]
buttocks [slang]	sentadera / nalgas [culo]	(SEHN-TAH-DEH-RAH) / (NAHL-GAHS) [KOOH-LOH]
labia	labios	(LAH-BIH-YOHS)
penis [slang]	pene [verga]	(PEH-NEH) [VEHR-GAH]
rectum	recto	(REHK-TOH)
semen [slang]	semen [mecos]	(SEH-MEHN) [MEH-KOHS]
sexual organs	organos sexuales	(OHR-GAH-NOHS) (SEHK-SWAH-LEHS)
testicles [slang]	testicos [huevos]	(TEHS-TIH-KOHS) [WEH-VOHS]

ANATOMY (SEXUAL ORGANS) ——

English	Spanish	Pronounced
vagina [slang]	vagina [panocha] / [el chiquito]	(VAH-HIH-NAH) [PAH-NOH-CHAH] / [EHL] [CHIH-KIH-TOH]

Terminology

— ANIMALS

English	Spanish	Pronounced
animal	animal	(AH-NIH-MAHL)
ant	hormiga	(OHR-MIH-GAH)
bear	oso	(OH-SOH)
bee	aveja	(AH-VEH-HAH)
bird	pajaro	(PAH-HAH-ROH)
bull	toro	(TOH-ROH)
cat	gato	(GAH-TOH)
chick	pollito	(POH-YIH-TOH)
chicken	gallina / pollo	(GAH-YIH-NAH) / (POH-YOH)
cow	vaca	(VAH-KAH)
dog	perro	(PEH-RROH)
eagle	aguila	(AH-GIH-LAH)
elephant	elefante	(EH-LEH-FAHN-TEH)
fish	pez / pescado	(PEHS) / (PEHS-KAH-DOH)
flea	pulga	(POOHL-GAH)
fox	zorra	(SOH-RRAH)

ANIMALS ——

English	Spanish	Pronounced
goat	cabra	(KAH-BRAH)
horse	caballo	(KAH-BAH-YOH)
insect	insecto	(IHN-SEHK-TOH)
lice	piojo / liendre	(PIH-YOH-HOH) / (LIH-YEHN-DREH)
lion	lion	(LEH-YOHN)
monkey	mono / chango	(MOH-NOH) / (CHAHN-GOH)
mouse	raton	(RAH-TOHN)
mule	mula	(MOOH-LAH)
opossum	tacuache	(TAH-KWAH-CHEH)
owl	tecolote / buho	(TEH-KOH-LOH-TEH) / (BOOH-OH)
ox	buey	(BOOH-WEHY)
parrot	perico / loro	(PEH-RIH-KOH) / (LOH-ROH)
pigeon [slang]	paloma [pichon]	(PAH-LOH-MAH) [PIH-CHOHN]

— ANIMALS

English	Spanish	Pronounced
raccoon	tejon / mapache	(TEH-HOHN) / (MAH-PAH-CHEH)
rat	rata	(RAH-TAH)
scorpion	escorpion / alacran	(EHS-KOHR-PIH-YOHN) / (AH-LAH-KRAHN)
sea gull	gaviota	(GAH-VIH-YOH-TAH)
serpent	serpiente	(SEHR-PIH-YEHN-TEH)
sheep	oveja	(OH-VEH-HAH)
skunk	zorrillo	(SOH-RRIH-YOH)
snake	vibora	(VIH-BOH-RAH)
spider	araña	(AH-RAH-NYAH)
tiger	tigere	(TIH-GEH-REH)
wasp	avispa	(AH-VIHS-PAH)
wolf	lobo	(LOH-BOH)

ARREST ——

English	Spanish	Pronounced
arrested	arrestado	(AH-RREHS-TAH-DOH)
detained	detenido	(DEH-TEH-NIH-DOH)
identified	identificado	(IH-DEHN-TIH-FIH-KAH-DOH)
ticket [slang]	infraccion / boleto [tikete]	(IHN-FRAHK-SYON) / (BOH-LEH-TOH) [TIH-KEH-TEH]
warning	aviso	(AH-VIH-SOH)
warrant	mandato / comprobante	(MAHN-DAH-TOH) / (KOHM-PROH-BAHN-TEH)

Terminology

— Clothing

English	Spanish	Pronounced
belt	cinto / faja	(SIHN-TOH) / (FAH-HAH)
boots	botas	(BOH-TAHS)
bracelet	pulsera	(POOHL-SEH-RAH)
cap	cachucha	(KAH-CHOOH-CHAH)
clothing	ropa	(ROH-PAH)
dress	vestido	(VEHS-TIH-DOH)
earrings	aretes	(AH-REH-TEHS)
glasses [slang]	lentes / anteojos [gafas]	(LEHN-TEHS) / (AHN-TEH-OH-HOHS) [GAH-FAHS]
gloves	guantes	(WAHN-TEHS)
hat [slang]	sombrero [tando]	(SOHM-BREH-ROH) [TAHN-DOH]
heels	tacones	(TAH-KOH-NEHS)
jacket	chaqueta	(CHAH-KEH-TAH)
jewelry	joyas	(HOH-YAHS)
necklace	collar	(KOH-YAHR)

CLOTHING —

English	Spanish	Pronounced
pants [slang]	pantalones [estramos] / [tramados]	(PAHN-TAH-LOH-NEHS) [EHS-TRAH-MOHS] / [TRAH-MAH-DOHS]
raincoat	capa	(KAH-PAH)
ring	anillo	(AH-NIH-YOH)
shirt [slang]	camisa [lisa]	(KAH-MIH-SAH) [LIH-SAH]
shoes [slang]	zapatos [calcos]	(SAH-PAH-TOHS) [KAHL-KOHS]
skirt	falda	(FAHL-DAH)
socks	calcetines	(KAHL-SEH-TIH-NEHS)
towel	toalla	(TOH-WAH-YAH)
undergarments [slang]	ropa interior [calzon / calzoncillos]	(ROH-PAH) (IHN-TEH-RIH-YOHR) [KAHL-SOHN / KAHL-SOHN-SIH-YOHS]
uniform	uniforme	(OOH-NIH-FOHR-MEH)
watch	reloj	(REH-LOH)

Terminology

— COLORS

English	Spanish	Pronounced
colors	colores	(KOH-LOH-REHS)
black	negro / prieto	(NEH-GROH) / (PRIH-YEH-TOH)
blue	azul	(AH-SOOHL)
brown	cafe	(KAH-FEH)
gold	oro	(OH-ROH)
gray	gris	(GRIHS)
green	verde	(VEHR-DEH)

Colors —

English	Spanish	Pronounced
orange	anaranjado	(AH-NAH-RAHN-HAH-DOH)
pink	color de rosa	(KOH-LOHR) (DEH) (ROH-SAH)
purple	purpura / morado	(POOHR-POOH-RAH) / (MOH-RAH-DOH)
red	rojo / colorado	(ROH-HOH) / (KOH-LOH-RAH-DOH)
silver	plateado	(PLAH-TEH-YAH-DOH)
white	blanco	(BLAHN-KOH)
yellow	amarillo	(AH-MAH-RIH-YOH)

Terminology

— CRIMES

English	Spanish	Pronounced
accident	accidente	(AHK-SIH-DEHN-TEH)
aggravated	con agravante	(KOHN AH-GRAH-VAHN-TEH)
alarm	alarma	(AH-LAHR-MAH)
ambush	emboscada	(EHM-BOHS-KAH-DAH)
appeal	apelacion	(AH-PEH-LAH-SIH-YOHN)
arson [slang]	incendio malicioso [lumbre adrede / torchada]	(IHN-SEHN-DIH-YOH) (MAH-LIH-SIH-YOH-SOH) [LOOHM-BREH] [AH-DREH-DEH] / [TOHR-CHAH-DAH]
assault	asalto	(AH-SAHL-TOH)
bail/bond	fianza	(FIH-YAHN-SAH)
blackmail	chantaje	(CHAHN-TAH-HEH)
blame	culpa	(KOOHL-PAH)
bomb	bomba	(BOHM-BAH)

CRIMES ——

English	Spanish	Pronounced
booked	fichado	(FIH-CHAH-DOH)
burglary [slang]	robo/ allanamiento [bogla]	(ROH-BOH / AH-YAH-NAH-MIH-YEHN-TOH) [BOHG-LAH]
(to) catch	pescar	(PEHS-KAHR)
charges	cargos	(KAHR-GOHS)
cheater [slang]	chapusero [chirion]	(CHAH-POOH-SEH-ROH) [CHIH-RIH-YOHN]
child abuse	malos tratos a un menor	(MAH-LOHS TRAH-TOHS AH OOHN MEH-NOHR)
complaint	queja	(KEH-HAH)
confiscate	confiscar	(KOHN-FIHS-KAHR)
criminal mischief	travesura criminal	(TRAH-VEH-SOOH-RAH) (KRIH-MIH-NAHL)
(to) cut	cortar	(KOHR-TAHR)
danger	peligro	(PEH-LIH-GROH)

Terminology

— CRIMES

English	Spanish	Pronounced
(to) deceive	engañar	(EHN-GAH-NYAHR)
details	detalles	(DEH-TAH-YEHS)
disguise	disfraz	(DIHS-FRAHS)
disorderly conduct	desorden publico	(DEHS-OHR-DEHN POOH-BLIH-KOH)
drug addict	drogadicto	(DROH-GAH-DIHK-TOH)
drugs	drogas	(DROH-GAHS)
drunk	borracho	(BOH-RRAH-CHOH)
DWI	manejando intoxicado	(MAH-NEH-HAHN-DOH) (IHN-TOHK-SIH-KAH-DOH)
DWLS	manejando con licensia suspendida	(MAH-NEH-HAHN-DOH) (KOHN) (LIH-SEHN-SIH-YAH) (SUHS-PEHN-DIH-DAH)
escape	escapar	(EHS-KAH-PAHR)
evidence	prueba	(PROOH-WEH-BAH)

CRIMES ——

English	Spanish	Pronounced
family violence	violencia familiar	(VIH-YOH-LEHN-SIH-YAH) (FAH-MIH-LIH-YAHR)
fault	culpa	(KOOHL-PAH)
felony [slang]	delito/ crimen mayor [felonia]	(DEH-LIH-TOH) / (KRIH-MEHN) (MAH-YOHR) [FEH-LOH-NIH-YAH]
fingerprints	huellas digitales	(HWEH-YAHS) (DIH-HIH-TAH-LEHS)
fire	lumbre	(LOOHM-BREH)
fondle	manosear	(MAH-NOH-SEH-YAHR)
forgery	falsificacion	(FAHL-SIH-FIH-KAH-SIH-YOHN)
frisk	esculcar	(EHS-KOOHL-KAHR)
fugitive	fugitivo	(FOOH-HIH-TIH-VOH)
gambling	tahureria / juegos de suerte	(TAH-OOH-REH-RIH-YAH) / (HWEH-GOHS) (DEH) (SOOH-WEHR-TEH)
gangs [slang]	pandillas [gangas]	(PAHN-DIH-YAHS) [GAHN-GAHS]

Terminology

— CRIMES

English	Spanish	Pronounced
hanged	colgado	(KOHL-GAH-DOH)
harass [slang]	hostigar [molestar]	(OHS-TIH-GAHR) [MOH-LEHS-TAHR]
hit & run	atropello y huido	(AH-TROH-PEH-YOH) (EE) (OOH-YIH-DOH)
homicide	homicidio	(OH-MIH-SIH-DIH-YOH)
homosexual [slang male] [" male] [" female]	homosexual [joto] [maricon] [mamflora]	(OH-MOH-SEHK-SWAHL) [HOH-TOH] [MAH-RIH-KOHN] [MAHM-FLOH-RAH]
injured	herido	(EH-RIH-DOH)
instigator	alcahuete / alborotador	(AHL-KAH-WEH-TEH) / (AHL-BOH-ROH-TAH-DOHR)
jail [slang]	carcel [el bote / calabozo]	(KAHR-SEHL) [EHL] [BOH-TEH] / [KAH-LAH-BOH-SOH]
jealousy	celos	(SEH-LOHS)

CRIMES ——

English	Spanish	Pronounced
juvenile delinquent	delincuente menor de edad	(DEH-LIHN-DWEHN-TEH) (MEH-NOHR) (DEH) (EH-DAHD)
kidnap	secuestro	(SEH-KWEHS-TROH)
laws	leyes	(LEH-YEHS)
liar [slang]	mentiroso [embustero]	(MEHN-TIH-ROH-SOH) [EHM-BOOHS-TEH-ROH]
misdemeanor	falto / crimen menor	(FAHL-TOH) / (KRIH-MEHN) (MEH-NOHR)
money	dinero	(DIH-NEH-ROH)
motive	motivo	(MOH-TIH-VOH)
murder / assassinate	asesinato	(AH-SEH-SIH-NAH-TOH)
narcotics	narcoticos	(NAHR-KOH-TIH-KOHS)
noise	ruido	(ROOH-IH-DOH)
nude [slang]	desnudo [encuerado]	(DEHS-NOOH-DOH) [EHN-KWEH-RAH-DOH]

Terminology

— CRIMES

English	Spanish	Pronounced
oath	juramento	(HOOH-RAH-MEHN-TOH)
obstruct	obstruir	(OHB-STROOH-IHR)
offenses	ofensas	(OH-FEHN-SAHS)
owner	dueño	(DWEH-NYOH)
paraphernalia	atavios	(AH-TAH-VIH-YOHS)
parole [slang]	licenciamento [cola]	(LIH-SEHN-SIH-YAH-MEHN-TOH) [KOH-LAH]
partners	compañeros	(KOHM-PAH-NYEH-ROHS)
peckerwood	chuntaro	(CHOOHN-TAH-ROH)
Peeping Tom	fizgon	(FIHS-GOHN)
penetrate	penetro	(PEH-NEH-TROH)
prison [slang]	prision [la pinta]	(PRIH-SIH-YOHN) [LAH] [PIHN-TAH]
prisoner	prisionero	(PRIH-SIH-YOH-NEH-ROH)

CRIMES ——

English	Spanish	Pronounced
problem	problema	(PROH-BLEH-MAH)
prostitution [slang]	prostitucion [putear]	(PROHS-TIH-TOOH-SIH-YOHN) [POOH-TYAHR]
provoke	provocar	(PROH-VOH-KAHR)
prowler / intruder	intruso	(IHN-TROOH-SOH)
punishment	castigo	(KAHS-TIH-GOH)
raped [slang]	violada [rapiada]	(VIH-YOH-LAH-DAH) [REH-IH-PYAH-DAH]
reason	razon	(RAH-SOHN)
regulation	reglamento	(REH-GLAH-MEHN-TOH)
report	reporte	(REH-POHR-TEH)
robbery	robo	(ROH-BOH)
runaway	huido	(OOH-IH-DOH)

Terminology

— CRIMES

English	Spanish	Pronounced
search	registro	(REH-HIHS-TROH)
(to) seize	incautacion / embargo	(IHN-KAH-OOH-TAH-SIH-YOHN) / (EHM-BAHR-GOH)
self defense	defensa propia	(DEH-FEHN-SAH) (PROH-PIH-YAH)
sentence	sentencia	(SEHN-TEHN-SIH-YAH)
sex	sexo	(SEHK-SOH)
shooting	balaseada / tiroteo	(BAH-LAH-SEH-YAH-DAH) / (TIH-ROH-TEH-YOH)
shoplifting	robo de tienda	(ROH-BOH) (DEH) (TIH-YEHN-DAH)
sick	enfermo	(EHN-FEHR-MOH)
sodomy	sodomia	(SOH-DOH-MIH-YAH)
strike	huelga	(OOH-WEHL-GAH)
suicide	suicido	(SOOH-IH-SIH-DOH)
suspect / suspicious	sospechoso	(SOHS-PEH-CHOH-SOH)

CRIMES ——

English	Spanish	Pronounced
theft	hurto/robo	(OOHR-TOH) / (ROH-BOH)
threat	amenaza	(AH-MEH-NAH-SAH)
ticket [slang]	infraccion / boleto [tikete]	(IHN-FRAHK-SIH-YOHN) / (BOH-LEH-TOH) [TIH-KEH-TEH]
traffic	trafico	(TRAH-FIH-KOH)
trespassing	traspasar	(TRAHS-PAH-SAHR)
troublemaker	alborotador	(AHL-BOH-ROH-TAH-DOHR)
vandalism [slang]	daños [vandalismo]	(DAH-NYOHS) [VAHN-DAH-LIHS-MOH]
wanted	fugitivo	(FOOH-HIH-TIH-VOH)
warning	aviso / alerta	(AH-VIH-SOH) / (AH-LEHR-TAH)
witness	testigo	(TEHS-TIH-GOH)
women's shelter	refugio de mujeres	(REH-FOOH-HYOH) (DEH) (MOOH-HEH-REHS)

Terminology

— DIRECTIONS

English	Spanish	Pronounced
down	abajo	(AH-BAH-HOH)
east	este / oriente	(EHS-TEH) / (OH-RIH-YEHN-TEH)
front	frente	(FREHN-TEH)
inside	adentro	(AH-DEHN-TROH)
left	izquierda	(IHS-KYEHR-DAH)
north	norte	(NOHR-TEH)
outside	afuera	(AH-FWEH-RAH)
over	sobre	(SOH-BREH)
rear	atras	(AH-TRAHS)
right	derecha	(DEH-REH-CHA)
south	sur	(SOOHR)
under	debajo	(DEH-BAH-HOH)
up	arriba	(AH-RRIH-BAH)
west	oeste / poniente	(OH-EHS-TEH) / (POH-NIH-YEHN-TEH)

DRUGS ——

English	Spanish	Pronounced
drugs	drogas	(DROH-GAHS)
beer [slang]	cerveza [pisto] / [vironga]	(SEHR-VEH-SAH) [PIHS-TOH] / [VIH-ROHN-GAH]
cigar	puro	(POOH-ROH)
cigarettes [slang]	cigarros [frajos]	(SIH-GAH-RROHS) [FRAH-HOHS]
cocaine [slang]	cocaina [coca] / [soda]	(KOH-KAH-IH-NAH) [KOH-KAH] / [SOH-DAH]
cooker [slang]	cocedor [cuca]	(KOH-SEH-DOHR) [KOOH-KAH]
drug gear [slang]	herramienta la "R"	(EH-RRAH-MIH-YEHN-TAH) [(LAH) (EH-RREH)]
heroin [slang]	heroina [carga] / [jale] / [mugrero] / [chiva]	(EH-ROH-IH-NAH) [KAHR-GAH] / [HAH-LEH] / [MOOH-GREH-ROH] / [CHIH-VAH]
liquor [slang]	licor [pisto]	(LIH-KOHR) [PIHS-TOH]

Terminology

— DRUGS

English	Spanish	Pronounced
marijuana [slang]	marijuana [mota] / [hierba]	(MAH-RIH-WAH-NAH) [MOH-TAH] / [YEHR-BAH]
pills	pildoras	(PIHL-DOH-RAHS)
syringe [slang]	jeringa [carabina]	(HEH-RIHN-GAH) [KAH-RAH-BIH-NAH]
wine	vino	(VIH-NOH)

47

FAMILY —

English	Spanish	Pronounced
family	familia	(FAH-MIH-LIH-YAH)
husband	esposo	(EHS-POH-SOH)
wife	esposa	(EHS-POH-SAH)
boyfriend	novio	(NOH-VIH-YOH)
girlfriend	novia	(NOH-VIH-YAH)
son	hijo	(IH-HOH)
daughter	hija	(IH-HAH)
children	niños	(NIH-NYOHS)
mother [slang]	madre / mama [jefa]	(MAH-DREH) / (MAH-MAH) [HEH-FAH]
father [slang]	padre / papa [jefe]	(PAH-DREH) / (PAH-PAH) [HEH-FEH]
parents	padres	(PAH-DREHS)
grandfather	abuelo	(AH-BWEH-LOH)
grandmother	abuela	(AH-BWEH-LAH)
brother [slang]	hermano [carnal]	(EHR-MAH-NOH) [KAHR-NAHL]

Terminology

— FAMILY

English	Spanish	Pronounced
sister [slang]	hermana [carnala]	(EHR-MAH-NAH) [KAHR-NAHL-LAH]
aunt	tia	(TIH-YAH)
uncle	tio	(TIH-YOH)
cousin	primo / prima	(PRI-MOH) / (PRI-MAH)
friend	amigo / amiga	(AH-MIH-GOH) / (AH-MIH-GAH)
neighbor	vecino / vecina	(VEH-SIH-NOH) / (VEH-SIH-NAH)
relative	pariente	(PAH-RIH-YEHN-TEH)
Mr.	Señor	(SEH-NYOHR)
Miss	Señorita	(SEH-NYOH-RIH-TAH)
Mrs.	Señora	(SEH-NYOH-RAH)
married	casado	(KAH-SAH-DOH)
divorced	divorciado	(DIH-VOHR-SYAH-DOH)
widowed	viuda	(VIH-YOOH-DAH)
engaged	comprometido	(KOHM-PROH-MEH-TIH-DOH)

GEMSTONES & PRECIOUS METALS —

English	Spanish	Pronounced
aquamarine	aquamarino	(AH-KWAH-MAH-RIH-NOH)
amethyst	amatista	(AH-MAH-TIHS-TAH)
brass	laton	(LAH-TOHN)
bronze	bronce	(BROHN-SEH)
chinaware	china	(CHIH-NAH)
copper	cobre	(KOH-BREH)
crystal	cristal	(KRIHS-TAHL)
diamond	diamante	(DIH-YAH-MAHN-TEH)
emerald	esmeralda	(EHS-MEH-RAHL-DAH)
garnet	garnet	(GAHR-NEHT)
glass	vidrio	(VIH-DRIH-YOH)
gold	oro	(OH-ROH)
ivory	marfil	(MAHR-FIHL)
leather	vaqueta	(VAH-KEH-TAH)
opal	opalo	(OH-PAH-LOH)
paper	papel	(PAH-PEHL)
pearl	perla	(PEHR-LAH)

Terminology

— GEMSTONES & PRECIOUS METALS

English	Spanish	Pronounced
pottery	ceramica / barro	(SEH-RAH-MIH-KAH) / (BAH-RROH)
rubber	goma / hule	(GOH-MAH) / (OOH-LEH)
ruby	rubi	(ROOH-BIH)
sapphire	zafiro	(SAH-FIH-ROH)
silk	seda	(SEH-DAH)
silver	plata	(PLAH-TAH)
tin	estaño / lata	(EHS-TAH-NYOH) / (LAH-TAH)
topaz	topacio	(TOH-PAH-SIH-YOH)
turquoise	turquesa	(TOOHR-KEH-SAH)
wood	madera / palo	(MAH-DEH-RAH) / (PAH-LOH)
zircon	zirconio	(SIHR-KOH-NYOH)

ILLNESSES & INJURIES —

English	Spanish	Pronounced
AIDS	SIDA	(SIH-DAH)
alive	vivo	(VIH-VOH)
asleep	dormido	(DOHR-MIH-DOH)
ambulance	ambulancia	(AHM-BOOH-LAHN-SIH-YAH)
awake	despierto	(DEHS-PIH-YEHR-TOH)
beaten [slang]	golpeado [stampado]	(GOHL-PEH-YAH-DOH) [STAHM-PAH-DOH]
blood	sangre	(SAHN-GREH)
castrated	capado	(KAH-PAH-DOH)
chicken pox	viruela	(VIH-ROOH-WEH-LAH)
clinic	clinica	(KLIH-NIH-KAH)
crazy [slang]	loco [tonto / safado]	(LOH-KOH) [TOHN-TOH / SAH-FAH-DOH]
cut	cortado	(KOHR-TAH-DOH)
dead	muerto	(MOOH-WEHR-TOH)
doctor	doctor	(DOHK-TOHR)
dying	muriendo	(MOOH-RIH-YEHN-DOH)
epileptic	epileptico	(EH-PIH-LEHP-TIK-KOH)

Terminology

— ILLNESSES & INJURIES

English	Spanish	Pronounced
gunshot	balaso / tiro	(BAH-LAH-SOH) / (TIH-ROH)
hepatitis	hepatitis	(EH-PAH-TIH-TIHS)
hidden	escondido	(EHS-KOHN-DIH-DOH)
hospital	hospital	(OHS-PIH-TAHL)
hurt	lastimado	(LAHS-TIH-MAH-DOH)
lost	perdido	(PEHR-DIH-DOH)
measles	sarampion	(SAH-RAHM-PIH-YOHN)
menstruate [slang]	menstruacion [reglar]	(MEHNS-TROOH-WAH-SIH-YOHN) [REH-GLAHR]
mumps	paperas	(PAH-PEH-RAHS)
numb	dormido	(DOHR-MIH-DOH)
pain	dolor	(DOH-LOHR)
polio	polio	(POH-LIH-YOH)
pregnant [slang]	embarazada [esperando] / [pansona]	(EHM-BAH-RAH-SAH-DAH) [EHS-PEH-RAHN-DOH] / [PAHN-SOH-NAH]
pulse	pulso	(POOHL-SOH)
punch	golpe	(GOHL-PEH)

ILLNESSES & INJURIES ——

English	Spanish	Pronounced
rest	descansa	(DEHS-KAHN-SAH)
running	corriendo	(KOH-RRIH-YEHN-DOH)
sick	enfermo	(EHN-FEHR-MOH)
stabbed [slang]	apuñalado [picado / cortado]	(AH-POOH-NYAH-LAH-DOH) [PIH-KAH-DOH] / [KOHR-TAH-DOH]
straitjacket	camisa de fuerza	(KAH-MIH-SAH) (DEH) (FOOH-WEHR-SAH)
tetanus [slang]	tetano [mal de arco]	(TEH-TAH-NOH) [(MAHL) (DEH) (AHR-KOH)]
tuberculosis [slang]	tuberculosis [T.B.]	(TOOH-BEHR-KOOH-LOH-SIHS) [TEH BEH]
walking	caminando	(KAH-MIH-NAHN-DOH)
wound	herida	(EH-RIH-DAH)

Terminology

— INTERROGATIVES

English	Spanish	Pronounced
again	otra vez	(OH-TRAH) (VEHS)
here	aqui	(AH-KIH)
how	como	(KOH-MOH)
how many	cuantos	(KWAHN-TOHS)
maybe [slang]	quizas [a lo mejor]	(KIH-SAHS) [(AH) (LOH) (MEH-HOHR)]
there	alli	(AH-YIH)
what	que	(KEH)
when	cuando	(KWAHN-DOH)
where	donde	(DOHN-DEH)
which	cual	(KWAHL)
who	quien	(KIH-YEHN)
why	porque	(POHR-KEH)

JEWELRY —

English	Spanish	Pronounced
jewelry	joyas	(HOH-YAHS)
belt	cinto / faja	(SIHN-TOH) / (FAH-HAH)
bracelet	pulsera	(POOHL-SEH-RAH)
buckle	hebilla	(EH-BIH-YAH)
earrings	aretes	(AH-REH-TEHS)
headband	cabezada	(KAH-BEH-SAH-DAH)
necklace	collar	(KOH-YAHR)
pendant	pendiente	(PEHN-DIH-YEHN-TEH)
pin	prendedor	(PREHN-DEH-DOHR)
pocket watch	reloj de bolsa	(REH-LOH) (DEH) (BOHL-SAH)
ring	anillo	(AH-NIH-YOH)
watch	reloj	(REH-LOH)

—— MANNERS

English	Spanish	Pronounced
again	otra vez	(OH-TRAH) (VEHS)
excuse me	dispensame	(DIHS-PEHN-SAH-MEH)
forgive me	disculpame	(DIHS-KOOHL-PAH-MEH)
gift	regalo	(REH-GAH-LOH)
God bless you	Dios te bendiga	(DIH-YOHS) (TEH) (BEHN-DIH-GAH)
good day	buen dia	(BWEHN) (DIH-YAH)
good morning	buenos dias	(BWEH-NOHS) (DIH-YAHS)
good evening	buenas tardes	(BWEH-NAHS) (TAHR-DEHS)
good night	buenas noches	(BWEH-NAHS) (NOH-CHEHS)
goodbye	adios	(AH-DIH-YOHS)
hello	hola	(OH-LAH)
I am officer	yo soy el official	(YOH) (SOHY) (EHL) (OH-FIH-SIH-YAHL)
I like it	me gusta	(MEH) (GOOHS-TAH)
no	no	(NOH)

MANNERS ——

English	Spanish	Pronounced
our condolences	nuestro pesame	(NWEHS-TROH) (PEH-SAH-MEH)
pardon me	perdoname	(PEHR-DOH-NAH-MEH)
please	por favor	(POHR) (FAH-VOHR)
some other time	alguna otra vez	(AHL-GOOH-NAH) (OH-TRAH) (VEHS)
thank you	gracias	(GRAH-SIH-YAHS)
a toast	un brindis	(OOHN) (BRIHN-DIHS)
very good	muy bien	(MOOH-IH) (BIH-YEHN)
with respect	con respeto	(KOHN) (REHS-PEH-TOH)
with your permission	con su permiso	(KOHN) (SOOH) (PEHR-MIH-SOH)
yes	si	(SIH)
you're welcome	de nada	(DEH) (NAH-DAH)

Terminology

—— MISCELLANOUS

English	Spanish	Pronounced
ashes	ceniza	(SEH-NIH-SAH)
bar	cantina	(KAHN-TIH-NAH)
beer	cerveza	(SEHR-VEH-SAH)
book	libro	(LIH-BROH)
box	caja	(KAH-HAH)
brush	cepillo	(SEH-PIH-YOH)
camera	camara	(KAH-MAH-RAH)
can	bote / lata	(BOH-TEH) / (LAH-TAH)
cassette	caset	(KAH-SEHT)
cassette player	casetera	(KAH-SEH-TEH-RAH)
citizen	cuidadano	(SOOH-WIH-DAH-DAH-NOH)
cloud	nube	(NOOH-BEH)
coffee [slang]	cafe [guariche]	(KAH-FEH) [WAH-RIH-CHEH]
cold	frio	(FRIH-YOH)
comb	peine	(PEH-IH-NEH)
computer	computadora	(KOHM-POOH-TAH-DOH-RAH)

MISCELLANOUS ——

English	Spanish	Pronounced
conversation	conversacion / platica	(KOHN-VEHR-SAH-SIH-YOHN) / (PLAH-TIH-KAH)
cool	fresco	(FREHS-KOH)
cooperate [slang]	cooperar [capear]	(KOH-OH-PEH-RAHR) [KAH-PEH-YAHR]
copy	copia	(KOH-PYAH)
cue stick	taco	(TAH-KOH)
dance	baile	(BAH-IH-LEH)
dirt	tierra	(TIH-YEH-RRAH)
distance	distancia	(DIHS-TAHN-SIH-YAH)
ditch [slang]	zanja [diche]	(SAHN-HAH) [DIH-CHEH]
dominoes	domino	(DOH-MIH-NOH)
drum	tambor	(TAHM-BOHR)
drunk	borracho	(BOH-RRAH-CHOH)
fire	lumbre / fuego	(LOOHM-BREH) / (FWEH-GOH)
fireman [slang]	bombero [lumbrero]	(BOHM-BEH-ROH) [LOOHM-BREH-ROH]

Terminology

— MISCELLANEOUS

English	Spanish	Pronounced
food [slang]	comida [refin]	(KOH-MIH-DAH) [REH-FIHN]
foreigner	fuereño	(FWEH-REH-NYOH)
furniture	muebles	(MWEH-BLEHS)
game	juego	(HOOH-WEH-GOH)
gasoline	gasolina	(GAH-SOH-LIH-NAH)
(to) get [slang]	coger / obtener [pañar]	(KOH-HEHR) / (OHB-TEH-NEHR) [PAH-NYAHR]
go	vete	(VEH-TEH)
good [slang]	bueno [de aquella / a toda madre/ a todo dar]	BWEH-NOH [(DEH) (AH-KEH-YAH) / (AH) (TOH-DAH) (MAH-DREH) / (AH) (TOH-DOH) (DAHR)]
government	gobierno	(GOH-BIH-YEHR-NOH)
guitar	gitarra	(GIH-TAH-RRAH)
hairbrush	cepillo	(SEH-PIH-YOH)
hate	odio	(OH-DIH-YOH)
hosiery	medias	(MEH-DIH-YAHS)

MISCELLANOUS ——

English	Spanish	Pronounced
hot	caliente	(KAH-LIH-YEHN-TEH)
kiss	beso	(BEH-SOH)
legend	leyenda	(LEH-YEHN-DAH)
like	gusta	(GOOHS-TAH)
(a) little	poquito	(POH-KIH-TOH)
long	largo	(LAHR-GOH)
(a) lot	mucho	(MOOH-CHOH)
love	amor / querer	(AH-MOHR) / (KEH-REHR)
matches [slang]	cerillos [trolas]	(SEH-RIH-YOHS) [TROH-LAHS]
money [slang]	dinero [feria / lana / verde / paca]	(DIH-NEH-ROH) [(FEH-RIH-YAH)/(LAH-NAH)/ (VEHR-DEH)/(PAH-KAH)]
moon	luna	(LOOH-NAH)
nap	siesta	(SIH-YEHS-TAH)
newspaper	periodico	(PEH-REH-YOH-DIH-KOH)
paintbrush	pincel	(PIHN-SEHL)
paper	papel	(PAH-PEHL)

— MISCELLANEOUS

English	Spanish	Pronounced
party	fiesta	(FIH-YEHS-TAH)
pen	pluma	(PLOOH-MAH)
pencil	lapiz	(LAH-PIHS)
photograph	fotografia	(FOH-TOH-GRAH-FIH-YAH)
picture	retrato	(REH-TRAH-TOH)
plate	plato	(PLAH-TOH)
playing cards	baraja	(BAH-RAH-HAH)
pliers	pinzas	(PIHN-SAHS)
poison	veneno	(VEH-NEH-NOH)
pool table	mesa de billar	(MEH-SAH) (DEH) (BIH-YAHR)
pool	alberca	(AHL-BEHR-KAH)
practice	practica / ensallo	(PRAHK-TIH-KAH) / (EHN-SAH-YOH)
pretty	bonita	(BOH-NIH-TAH)
question	pregunta	(PREH-GOOHN-TAH)
radar	radar	(RAH-DAHR)
radio	radio	(RAH-DIH-YOH)
rain	lluvia	(YOOH-VIH-YAH)

MISCELLANOUS ——

English	Spanish	Pronounced
record	registro / discos	(REH-HIHS-TROH) / (DIHS-KOHS)
record player	toca discos	(TOH-KAH) (DIHS-KOHS)
sand	arena	(AH-REH-NAH)
scaffold	andamio	(AHN-DAH-MIH-YOH)
signal	señal	(SEH-NYAHL)
sky	cielo	(SIH-YEH-LOH)
(to) smoke	fumar	(FOOH-MAHR)
social security number	numero de seguro social	(NOOH-MEH-ROH) (DEH) (SEH-GOOH-ROH) (SOH-SIH-YAHL)
stereo	estereo	(EHS-TEH-REH-YOH)
sun	sol	(SOHL)
sweet 15 / debutante	quinceañera	(KIHN-SEH-AH-NYEH-RAH)
telephone	telefono	(TEH-LEH-FOH-NOH)
television	televisor	(TEH-LEH-VIH-SOHR)
(# of) times	veces	(VEH-SEHS)

Terminology

— MISCELLANEOUS

English	Spanish	Pronounced
tools [slang]	herramienta [fierros]	(EH-RRAH-MIH-YEHN-TAH) [FIH-YEH-RROHS]
trash	basura	(BAH-SOOH-RAH)
trumpet	trompeta	(TROHM-PEH-TAH)
ugly	feo	(FEH-YOH)
VCR	video casetera	(VIH-DIH-YOH) (KAH-SEH-TEH-RAH)
visitor	visitante	(VIH-SIH-TAHN-TEH)
water hose	manguera	(MAHN-GEH-RAH)
wedding	boda	(BOH-DAH)
what's up	que pasa / que honda	(KEH) (PAH-SAH) / (KEH) (OHN-DAH)
breakfast	almuerzo	(AHL-MOOH-WEHR-SOH)
lunch	merienda / comida	(MEH-RIH-YEHN-DAH) / (KOH-MIH-DAH)
dinner	comida	(KOH-MIH-DAH)
supper	cena	(SEH-NAH)

MONEY —

English	Spanish	Pronounced
money [slang]	dinero [feria / lana / paca / verde]	(DIH-NEH-ROH) [FEH-RIH-YAH / LAH-NAH / PAH-KAH / VEHR-DEH]
dollar [peso sometimes]	dolar [peso]	(DOH-LAHR) [PEH-SOH]
silver dollar	dolar de plata	(DOH-LAHR) (DEH) (PLAH-TAH)
50¢ piece [slang]	toston [tolon]	(TOHS-TOHN) [TOH-LOHN]
quarter [slang]	peseta [quira]	(PEH-SEH-TAH) [KWIH-RAH]
bit (2 bits = 25¢)	real	(RREH-YAHL)
dime [slang]	diez centavos [dimo/dyme]	(DIH-YEHS) (SEHN-TAH-VOHS) [DIH-MOH / DY-MEH]
nickel [slang]	cinco centavos [nicle]	(SIHN-KOH) (SEHN-TAH-VOHS) [NIH-KLEH]
penny	centavo	(SEHN-TAH-VOH)
check	cheque	(CHEH-KEH)

Terminology

— MONEY

English	Spanish	Pronounced
credit	credito	(KREH-DIH-TOH)
credit card	tarjeta de credito	(TAHR-HEH-TAH) (DEH) (KREH-DIH-TOH)
loan	prestamo	(PREHS-TAH-MOH)
money order	giro postal	(HIH-ROH) (POHS-TAHL)

NUMBERS —

English	Spanish	Pronounced
numbers	numeros	(NOOH-MEH-ROHS)
0	cero	(SEH-ROH)
1	uno	(OOH-NOH)
2	dos	(DOHS)
3	tres	(TREHS)
4	cuatro	(KWAH-TROH)
5	cinco	(SIN-KOH)
6	seiz	(SAYS)
7	siete	(SIH-YEH-TEH)
8	ocho	(OH-CHOH)
9	nueve	(NOOH-WEH-VEH)
10	diez	(DIH-YEHS)

Terminology

— NUMBERS

English	Spanish	Pronounced
11	once	(OHN-SEH)
12	doce	(DOH-SEH)
13	trece	(TREH-SEH)
14	catorce	(KAH-TOHR-SEH)
15	quince	(KIHN-SEH)
16	diez y seiz	(DIH-YEHS) (EE) (SAYS)
17	diez y siete	(DIH-YEHS) (EE) (SIH-YEH-TEH)
18	diez y ocho	(DIH-YEHS) (EE) (OH-CHOH)
19	diez y nueve	(DIH-YEHS) (EE) (NOOH-WEH-VEH)
20	veinte	(VEH-IHN-TEH)
21	veinte y uno	(VEH-IHN-TEH) (EE) (OOH-NOH)
30	treinta	(TREH-IHN-TAH)
40	cuarenta	(KOOH-WAH-REHN-TAH)

NUMBERS ——

English	Spanish	Pronounced
50	cincuenta	(SIHN-KWEHN-TAH)
60	sesenta	(SEH-SEHN-TAH)
70	setenta	(SEH-TEHN-TAH)
80	ochenta	(OH-CHEHN-TAH)
90	noventa	(NOH-VEHN-TAH)
100	cien	(SIH-YEHN)
500	quinientos	(KIH-NIH-YEHN-TOHS)
1000	mil	(MIHL)
thousands	miles	(MIH-LEHS)
millions	millones	(MIH-YOH-NEHS)

—— OCCULT

English	Spanish	Pronounced
angel	angel	(AHN-HEHL)
bible	biblia	(BIH-BLIH-YAH)
black magic	magia negra	(MAH-HIH-YAH) (NEH-GRAH)
candle	vela	(VEH-LAH)
curse	maldicion	(MAHL-DIH-SIH-YOHN)
demon	demonio	(DEH-MOH-NIH-YOH)
devil [slang]	diablo [paulin]	(DIH-YAH-BLOH) [PAH-OOH-LIHN]
enchantment	encanto	(EHN-KAHN-TOH)
flying saucer	platillo volador	(PLAH-TIH-YOH) (VOH-LAH-DOHR)
ghost / phantom	fantasma	(FAHN-TAHS-MAH)
God	Dios	(DIH-YOHS)
healer	curandero	(KOOH-RAHN-DEH-ROH)
herbs	hierbas	(YEHR-BAHS)
hypnotize	hipnotizar	(IHP-NOH-TIH-SAHR)
incense	incienso	(IHN-SIH-YEHN-SOH)

OCCULT —

English	Spanish	Pronounced
Lucifer	Lucifer	(LOOH-SIH-FEHR)
mass	misa	(MIH-SAH)
magic	magia	(MAH-HIH-YAH)
miracle	milagro	(MIH-LAH-GROH)
powder	polvo	(POHL-VOH)
sacrifice	sacrificio	(SAH-KRIH-FIH-SIH-YOH)
saint	santo	(SAHN-TOH)
satan	satanas	(SAH-TAH-NAHS)
sleep walking	sonambulo	(SOH-NAHM-BOOH-LOH)
soul	alma	(AHL-MAH)
spell	hechizo	(EH-CHIH-SOH)
spirit	espirito	(EHS-PIH-RIH-TOH)
witch	bruja	(BROOH-HAH)
witchcraft	brujeria	(BROOH-HEH-RIH-YAH)

Terminology

—— OCCUPATIONS

English	Spanish	Pronounced
occupation	ocupacion	(OH-KOOH-PAH-SIH-YOHN)
job [slang]	empleo [cameo]	(EHM-PLEH-YOH) [KAH-MEH-YOH]
actor	actor	(AHK-TOHR)
agent	agente	(AH-HEHN-TEH)
artist	artista	(AHR-TIHS-TAH)
author	autor	(AH-OOH-TOHR)
baby sitter	nana / niñera	(NAH-NAH) / (NIH-NYEH-RAH)
barber	barbero	(BAHR-BEH-ROH)
boxer	boxeador	(BOKH-SEH-YAH-DOHR)
butcher	carnicero	(KAHR-NIH-SEH-ROH)
captain	capitan	(KAH-PIH-TAHN)
carpenter	carpintero	(KAHR-PIHN-TEH-ROH)
cashier	cajera	(KAH-HEH-RAH)
chauffeur	chófer	(CHOH-FEHR)
coach / trainer	entrenador	(EHN-TREH-NAH-DOHR)
colonel	coronel	(KOH-ROH-NEHL)

OCCUPATIONS ——

English	Spanish	Pronounced
cook	cocinero	(KOH-SIH-NEH-ROH)
coroner	medico forenso	(MEH-DIH-KOH) (FOH-REHN-SOH)
councilman	concejal	(KOHN-SEH-HAHL)
cowboy	vaquero	(VAH-KEH-ROH)
D.A. / prosecutor	fiscal	(FIHS-KAHL)
dancer	bailarina	(BAH-IH-LAH-RIH-NAH)
deputy	diputado	(DIH-POOH-TAH-DOH)
doctor	doctor / médico	(DOHK-TOHR) / (MEH-DIH-KOH)
dog catcher	perrero	(PEH-RREH-ROH)
driver	chófer	(CHOH-FEHR)
electrician	electricista	(EH-LEHK-TRIH-SIHS-TAH)
engineer	ingeniero	(IHN-HEH-NIH-YEH-ROH)
farmer	granjero	(GRAHN-HEH-ROH)
fireman	bombero / lumbrero	(BOHM-BEH-ROH) / (LOOHM-BREH-ROH)
fisherman	pescador	(PEHS-KAH-DOHR)

Terminology

— OCCUPATIONS

English	Spanish	Pronounced
gambler	tahur	(TAH-OOHRR)
general	general	(HEH-NEH-RAHL)
guard	guardia	(WAHR-DIH-YAH)
handicapped	inpedimentado	(IHM-PEH-DIH-MEHN-TAH-DOH)
housewife	ama de casa	(AH-MAH) (DEH) (KAH-SAH)
hunter	cazador	(KAH-SAH-DOHR)
inspector	inspector	(IHN-SPEHK-TOHR)
interpreter	intérprete	(IHN-TEHR-PREH-TEH)
janitor / porter	portero	(POHR-TEH-ROH)
judge	juez	(HOOH-WEHS)
laborer	obrero	(OH-BREH-ROH)
lawyer	abogado	(AH-BOH-GAH-DOH)
lieutenant	teniente	(TEH-NIH-YEHN-TEH)
magician	mago / magico	(MAH-GOH) / (MAH-HIH-KOH)
major	mayor	(MAH-YOHR)
mayor	alcalde	(AHL-KAHL-DEH)

OCCUPATIONS —

English	Spanish	Pronounced
manager	gerente	(HEH-REHN-TEH)
mechanic	mecánico	(MEH-KAH-NIH-KOH)
medic	medico	(MEH-DIH-KOH)
nun	monja	(MOHN-HAH)
nurse	enfermera	(EHN-FEHRR-MEH-RAH)
painter	pintor	(PIHN-TOHR)
photographer	fotógrafo	(FOH-TOH-GRAH-FOH)
pilot	piloto	(PIH-LOH-TOH)
plumber	plomero	(PLOH-MEH-ROH)
priest	padre / cura	(PAH-DREH) / (KOOH-RAH)
principal	principal	(PRIHN-SIH-PAHL)
rancher	ranchero	(RAHN-CHEH-ROH)
reporter	reportero	(REH-POHR-TEH-ROH)
representative	representante	(REH-PREH-SEHN-TAHN-TEH)
retired	retirado	(REH-TIH-RAH-DOH)
salesman	vendedor	(VEHN-DEH-DOHR)

Terminology

— OCCUPATIONS

English	Spanish	Pronounced
secretary	secretaria	(SEH-KREH-TAH-RIH-YAH)
sergeant	sargento	(SAHR-HEHN-TOH)
singer	cantor / cantante	(KAHN-TOHR) / (KAHN-TAHN-TEH)
soldier	soldado	(SOHL-DAH-DOH)
tailor	sastre	(SAHS-TREH)
teacher	maestra	(MAH-YEHS-TRAH)
tourist	turista	(TOOH-RIHS-TAH)
welder	soldador	(SOHL-DAH-DOHR)

PERSONS —

English	Spanish	Pronounced
man [slang]	hombre [ruco]	(OHM-BREH) [ROOH-KOH]
boy [slang]	niño / muchacho [werkito]	(NIH-NYOH) / (MOOH-CHAH-CHOH) [WEHR-KIH-TOH]
woman [slang]	mujer [ruca]	(MOOH-HEHR) [ROOH-KAH]
girl [slang]	niña / muchacha [werkita]	(NIH-NYAH) / (MOOH-CHAH-CHAH) [WEHR-KIH-TAH]
baby [slang]	bebe [criatura]	(BEH-BEH) [KRIH-YAH-TOOH-RAH]
age	edad	(EH-DAHD)
bachelor	soltero	(SOHL-TEH-ROH)
married	casado	(KAH-SAH-DOH)
divorced	divorciado	(DIH-VOHR-SIH-YAH-DOH)
common law married	casado a ley comun	(KAH-SAH-DOH) (AH) (LAY) (KOH-MOOHN)
couple / pair	pareja / par	(PAH-REH-HAH) / (PAHR)

Terminology

— PERSONS

English	Spanish	Pronounced
big	grande	(GRAHN-DEH)
little	chico / pequeño	(CHIH-KOH) / (PEH-KEH-NYOH)
light	liviano	(LIH-VIH-YAH-NOH)
heavy	pesado	(PEH-SAH-DOH)
tall	alto	(AHL-TOH)
short	bajo / chaparro	(BAH-HOH) / (CHAH-PAH-RROH)
giant	gigante	(HEEH-GAHN-TEH)
midget	enano	(EH-NAH-NOH)
long	largo	(LAHR-GOH)
thin	delgado / flaco	(DEHL-GAH-DOH) / (FLAH-KOH)
fat	gordo / panson	(GOHR-DOH) / (PAHN-SOHN)
shadow	sombra	(SOHM-BRAH)
white [slang]	blanco [gringo / guero / bolillo]	(BLAHN-KOH) [GRIHN-GOH / WEH-ROH / BOH-LIH-YOH]

PERSONS ——

English	Spanish	Pronounced
black [slang]	negro [mayate / grillo]	(NEH-GROH) / [MAH-YAH-TEH / GRIH-YOH]
Latin / Hispanic [slang]	Latino / Hispano [Mejicano / Chicano]	(LAH-TIH-NOH) / (IHS-PAH-NOH) [MEH-HIH-KAH-NOH / CHIH-KAH-NOH]
Chinese	Chino	(CHIH-NOH)
Indian	Indio	(IHN-DYOH)
Arab	Arabe	(AH-RAH-BEH)
Mr.	Señor	(SEH-NYOHR)
Mrs.	Señora	(SEH-NYOH-RAH)
Miss	Señorita	(SEH-NYOH-RIH-TAH)
name	nombre	(NOHM-BREH)
surname	apellido	(AH-PEH-YIH-DOH)

— POLICE

English	Spanish	Pronounced
police	policia / gendarme	(POH-LIH-SIH-YAH) / (HEHN-DAHR-MEH)
[slang]	[jurado / chota / policiano]	[HOOH-RAH-DOH / CHOH-TAH / POH-LIH-SIH-YAH-NOH]
The following may all be used to indicate uniformed officers		
dog [slang]	perro [perrado]	(PEH-RROH) [PEH-RRAH-DOH]
John	Juan	(HWAHN)
the law	la ley	(LAH) (LAY)
the blue one	el de azul	(EHL) (DEH) (AH-SOOHL)
the badge	la bacha	(LAH) (BAH-CHAH)
the one with the gun	el de la pistola	(EHL) (DEH) (LAH) (PIHS-TOH-LAH)

PROFANITY —

English	Spanish	Pronounced
ass	culo	(KOOH-LOH)
asshole	fondillo / jondillo / culero	(FOHN-DIH-YOH) / (HOHN-DIH-YOH) / (KOOH-LEH-ROH)
ass kisser / brown nose	besa culo / lambiache	(BEH-SAH KOOH-LOH) (LAHM-BIH-YAH-CHEH)
ass licker	lambe nalgas	(LAHM-BEH) (NAHL-GAHS)
bastard	bastardo	(BAHS-TAHR-DOH)
big shit	chingon	(CHIHN-GOHN)
bitch / whore	puto / puta	(POOH-TOH) / (POOH-TAH)
bitching / fucking	chingando	(CHIHN-GAHN-DOH)
breasts	chiches / tetas	(CHIH-CHEHS) / (TET-TAHS)
bullshitter	hablador	(AH-BLAH-DOHR)
buttocks	nalgas	(NAHL-GAHS)
cocksucker	mamalon / mamon / lambe huevos	(MAH-MAH-LOHN) / (MAH-MOHN) / (LAHM-BEH) (WEH-VOHS)
cunt / pussy	panocha / el chiquito	(PAH-NOH-CHAH) / (EHL) (CHIH-KIH-TOH)

— PROFANITY

English	Spanish	Pronounced
dick	verga / piruta / chorizo / picha	(VEHR-GAH) / (PIH-ROOH-TAH) / (CHOH-RIH-SOH) / (PIH-CHAH)
dumb ass	baboso	(BAH-BOH-SOH)
dumb shit	mayuga	(MAH-YOOH-GAH)
fag	joto / huizo / maricon	(HOH-TOH) / (WEE-SOH) / (MAH-RIH-KOHN)
fuck	coger	(KOH-HEHR)
fucked / damned	chingado	(CHIHN-GAH-DOH)
fuck your mother	chinga tu madre / tu jefa	(CHIHN-GAH) (TOOH) (MAH-DREH) / (TOOH) (HEH-FAH)
fuck your grandmother	chinga tu abuela	(CHIHN-GAH) (TOOH) (AH-WEH-LAH)
idiot	idiota	(IH-DIH-YOH-TAH)
imbecile	imbecil	(IHM-BEH-SIHL)
lesbian	jota / mamflora	(HOH-TAH) / (MAHM-FLOH-RAH)
jack-off	puñata / puñeta	(POOH-NYAH-TAH) / (POOH-NYEH-TAH)

PROFANITY ——

English	Spanish	Pronounced
loud mouth	hocicon	(OH-SIH-KOHN)
[damn] animal mouth	hocico	(OH-SIH-KOH)
motherfucker	cojemadre	(KOH-HEH-MAH-DREH)
shit	mierda / cagada / cuacha	(MIH-YEHR-DAH) / (KAH-GAH-DAH) / (KWAH-CHAH)
shithead	pendejo	(PEHN-DEH-HOH)
shitty / damned	pinche / gacho	(PIHN-CHEH) / (GAH-CHOH)
son of a bitch	hijo de puta	(IH-HOH) (DEH) (POOH-TAH)
stupid	estupido	(EHS-TOOH-PIH-DOH)
turd	mojon	(MOH-HOHN)

—— Senses

English	Spanish	Pronounced
senses	sentidos	(SEHN-TIH-DOHS)
eyesight	vista	(VIHS-TAH)
hearing	oir / escuchar	(OH-YIHR) / (EHS-KOOH-CHAHR)
touch	tocar / tentar	(TOH-KAHR) / (TEHN-TAHR)
smell	oler	(OH-LEHR)
taste	probar / saborear	(PROH-BAHR) / (SAH-BOH-REH-YAHR)
(to) watch	ver / vigilar	(VEHR) / (VIH-HIH-LAHR)
(to) yell	gritar	(GRIH-TAHR)
(to) lick [slang]	lamer [lambir]	(LAH-MEHR) [LAHM-BIHR]

STRUCTURES —

English	Spanish	Pronounced
alley	callejon	(KAH-YEH-HOHN)
apartments	apartamentos / departamentos	(AH-PAHR-TAH-MEHN-TOHS) / (DEH-PAHR-TAH-MEHN-TOHS)
bank	banco	(BAHN-KOH)
basement	sotano / subterraneo	(SOH-TAH-NOH) / (SOOHB-TEH-RRAH-NEH-YOH)
bathroom	baño	(BAH-NYOH)
bed	cama	(KAH-MAH)
bedroom	recamara	(REH-KAH-MAH-RAH)
block	cuadra	(KWAH-DRAH)
building	edificio	(EH-DIH-FIH-SIH-YOH)
carpet	carpeta	(KAHR-PEH-TAH)
chimney	chimenea	(CHIH-MEH-NEH-YAH)
church	iglesia	(IH-GLEH-SIH-YAH)
door	puerta	(PWEHR-TAH)
downstairs	piso de abajo	(PIH-SOH) (DEH) (AH-BAH-HOH)
fan	abanico	(AH-BAH-NIH-KOH)
fence	cerca	(SEHR-KAH)

Terminology

— STRUCTURES

English	Spanish	Pronounced
foundation	fundacion	(FOOHN-DAH-SIH-YOHN)
garage	garaje	(GAH-RAH-HEH)
gravel	grava	(GRAH-VAH)
hallway	pasadero	(PAH-SAH-DEH-ROH)
hole	hoyo / agujero	(OH-YOH) / (AH-GOOH-HEH-ROH)
hospital	hospital	(OHS-PIH-TAHL)
house	casa	(KAH-SAH)
kitchen	cocina	(KOH-SIH-NAH)
library	biblioteca	(BIH-BLIH-YOH-TEH-KAH)
light	luz	(LOOHS)
lights	luces	(LOOH-SEHS)
living room	sala	(SAH-LAH)
lumber	madera	(MAH-DEH-RAH)
mortuary	mortuaria	(MOOHR-TOOH-WAH-RIH-YAH)
neighborhood	vecindad	(VEH-SIHN-DAHD)
office	oficina	(OH-FIH-SIH-NAH)

STRUCTURES ──

English	Spanish	Pronounced
park	parque	(PAHR-KEH)
patio	patio	(PAH-TIH-YOH)
pillow	almohada	(AHL-MOH-WAH-DAH)
pillowcase	funda	(FOOHN-DAH)
pool	alberca	(AHL-BEHR-KAH)
porch [slang]	portal [galeria]	(POHR-TAHL) [GAH-LEH-RIH-YAH]
restaurant	restaurante	(REHS-TAH-OOH-RAHN-TEH)
roof	techo	(TEH-CHOH)
room	cuarto	(KWAHR-TOH)
rug	alfombra	(AHL-FOHM-BRAH)
sand	arena	(AH-REH-NAH)
school	escuela	(EHS-KWEH-LAH)
screen	tela	(TEH-LAH)
second floor	segundo piso	(SEH-GOOHN-DOH) (PIH-SOH)
stairs	escalones	(EHS-KAH-LOH-NEHS)
store	tienda	(TIH-YEHN-DAH)

Terminology

— STRUCTURES

English	Spanish	Pronounced
table	mesa	(MEH-SAH)
theatre	teatro	(TEH-YAH-TROH)
water	agua	(AH-GWAH)
window	ventana	(VEHN-TAH-NAH)
yard	yarda / solar	(YAHR-DAH) / (SOH-LAHR)

TIME —

English	Spanish	Pronounced
time	tiempo	(TIH-YEHM-POH)
now	ahorita	(AH-OH-RIH-TAH)
later	despues	(DEHS-PWEHS)
today	ahora	(AH-OH-RAH)
yesterday	ayer	(AH-YEHR)
last night	anoche	(AH-NOH-CHEH)
tomorrow	mañana	(MAH-NYAH-NAH)
year	año	(AH-NYOH)
month	mes	(MEHS)
day	dia	(DIH-YAH)
night	noche	(NOH-CHEH)
hour	hora	(OH-RAH)
minute	minuto	(MIH-NOOH-TOH)
second	segundo	(SEH-GOOHN-DOH)
quick	pronto	(PROHN-TOH)
slow	despacio	(DEHS-PAH-SIH-YOH)
dark	obscuro	(OHB-SKOOH-ROH)

Terminology

— TIME

English	Spanish	Pronounced
light	luz	(LOOHS)
Monday	Lunes	(LOOH-NEHS)
Tuesday	Martes	(MAHR-TEHS)
Wednesday	Miercoles	(MIH-YEHR-KOH-LEHS)
Thursday	Jueves	(HWEH-VEHS)
Friday	Viernes	(VIH-YEHR-NEHS)
Saturday	Sabado	(SAH-BAH-DOH)
Sunday	Domingo	(DOH-MIHN-GOH)
January	Enero	(EH-NEH-ROH)
February	Febrero	(FEH-BREH-ROH)
March	Marzo	(MAHR-SOH)
April	Abril	(AH-BRIHL)
May	Mayo	(MAH-YOH)
June	Junio	(HOOH-NYOH)
July	Julio	(HOOH-LYOH)
August	Agosto	(AH-GOHS-TOH)
September	Septiembre	(SEHP-TIH-YEHM-BREH)

TIME ——

English	Spanish	Pronounced
October	Octubre	(OHK-TOOH-BREH)
November	Noviembre	(NOH-VIH-YEHM-BREH)
December	Diciembre	(DIH-SIH-YEHM-BREH)
spring	primavera	(PRIH-MAH-VEH-RAH)
summer	verano	(VEH-RAH-NOH)
fall	otoño	(OH-TOH-NYOH)
winter	invierno	(IHN-VIH-YEHR-NOH)

Terminology

— VEHICLES

English	Spanish	Pronounced
airplane	avion / aeroplano	(AH-VIH-YOHN) / (AH-EH-ROH-PLAH-NOH)
ambulance	ambulancia	(AHM-BOOH-LAHN-SIH-YAH)
bicycle	bicicleta	(BIH-SIH-KLEH-TAH)
boat	barco / lancha	(BAHR-KOH) / (LAHN-CHAH)
bus	autobus / camion	(OW-TOH-BOOHS) / (KAH-MYOHN)
cab / taxi	coche / taxi	(KOH-CHEH) / (TAHK-SIH)
car	carro	(KAH-RROH)
motorcycle	motocicleta	(MOH-TOH-SIH-KLEH-TAH)
station wagon	camioneta	(KAH-MYOH-NEH-TAH)
tractor	tractor	(TRAHK-TOHR)
trailer	treila	(TREH-IH-LAH)
truck	troca / camion	(TROH-KAH) / (KAH-MYOHN)
van	camion	(KAH-MYOHN)

VEHICLES ——

English	Spanish	Pronounced
wrecker [slang]	grua [wrecka]	(GROOH-WAH) [REH-KAH]
abandoned	abandonado	(AH-BAHN-DOH-NAH-DOH)
brakes [slang]	frenos [manellas]	(FREH-NOHS) [MAH-NEH-YAHS]
bumper	defensa	(DEH-FEHN-SAH)
door	puerta	(PWEHR-TAH)
drive [slang]	conducir [manejar / arriar]	(KOHN-DOOH-SIHR) [MAH-NEH-HAHR / AH-RRIH-YAHR]
fender	polvera	(POHL-VEH-RAH)
hood	cubierta	(KOOH-BYEHR-TAH)
hub cap	tapa	(TAH-PAH)
inspection sticker	etiqueta de inspeccion	(EH-TIH-KEH-TAH) (DEH) (IHNS-PEHK-SYOHN)
keys	llaves	(YAH-VEHS)

Terminology

— VEHICLES

English	Spanish	Pronounced
license	licensia	(LIH-SEHN-SYAH)
motor/engine [slang]	motor [maquina]	(MOH-TOHR) [MAH-KIH-NAH]
muffler [slang]	silenciador [mofle]	(SIH-LEHN-SIH-YAH-DOHR) [MOH-FLEH]
(to) park [slang]	estacionar [parquear]	(EHS-TAH-SIH-YOH-NAHR) [PAHR-KEH-YAHR]
plates	placas	(PLAH-KAHS)
regular size	regular	(RREH-GOOH-LAHR)
rims	rines	(RRIH-NEHS)
roof	capasete	(KAH-PAH-SEH-TEH)
scraped	raspado	(RAHS-PAH-DOH)
small size	chico	(CHIH-KOH)
steering wheel	volante / manejera	(VOH-LAHN-TEH) / (MAH-NEH-HEH-RAH)

VEHICLES —

English	Spanish	Pronounced
tank	tanque	(TAHN-KEH)
tire	llanta	(YAHN-TAH)
transmission	transmision	(TRAHNS-MIH-SYOHN)
trunk [slang]	cajuela [castaña]	(KAH-HWEH-LAH) [KAHS-TAH-NYAH]
window	ventana	(VEHN-TAH-NAH)
windshield	parabrisa	(PAH-RAH-BRIH-SAH)
wrecked	chocado	(CHOH-KAH-DOH)

CHAPTER 2

Terminology

—— WEAPONS

English	Spanish	Pronounced
weapons	armas	(AHR-MAHS)
acid	acido	(AH-SIH-DOH)
ammunition	parque	(PAHR-KEH)
ax	acha	(AH-CHAH)
bomb	bomba	(BOHM-BAH)
bottle	botella	(BOH-TEH-YAH)
chain	cadena	(KAH-DEH-NAH)
club	garrote	(GAH-RROH-TEH)
dagger	daga / puñal	(DAH-GAH) / (POOH-NYAHL)
dynamite	dinamita	(DIH-NAH-MIH-TAH)
fire	lumbre	(LOOHM-BREH)
gas	gas	(GAHS)
glass	vidrio	(VIH-DRIH-YOH)
hammer	martillo	(MAHR-TIH-YOH)
handcuffs	esposas	(EHS-POH-SAHS)
hoe	asadon	(AH-SAH-DOHN)

WEAPONS ——

English	Spanish	Pronounced
knife [slang]	cuchillo [navaja / filero]	(KOOH-CHIH-YOH) [NAH-VAH-HAH / FIH-LEH-ROH]
knuckles	manopla	(MAH-NOH-PLAH)
machete	machete	(MAH-CHEH-TEH)
machine gun	ametralladora	(AH-MEH-TRAH-YAH-DOH-RAH)
nunchakus [slang]	nunchakus [palos chinos]	(NOOHN-CHAH-KOOHS) [(PAH-LOHS) (CHIH-NOHS)]
pick	talache	(TAH-LAH-CHEH)
pistol [slang]	pistola [cuhete / plomero / clicka]	(PIHS-TOH-LAH) [KWEH-TEH / PLOH-MEH-ROH / KLIH-KAH]
pitchfork	horquilla	(OHR-KIH-YAH)
rake	rastrillo	(RAHS-TRIH-YOH)
rifle [slang]	rifle [carabina]	(RIH-FLEH) [KAH-RAH-BIH-NAH]
rock	piedra	(PIH-YEH-DRAH)
rope	mecate	(MEH-KAH-TEH)

Terminology

— WEAPONS

English	Spanish	Pronounced
scissors	tijeras	(TIH-HEH-RAHS)
shoot [slang]	disparar / tirar [plomear / churear]	(DIHS-PAH-RAHR) / (TIH-RAHR) [PLOH-MEH-YAHR / CHOOH-REH-YAHR]
shotgun	escopeta	(EHS-KOH-PEH-TAH)
shovel	pala	(PAH-LAH)
spear	lanza	(LAHN-SAH)
steel toe	punta de fiero	(POOHN-TAH) (DEH) (FIH-YEH-ROH)
stick	palo	(PAH-LOH)
sword	espada	(EHS-PAH-DAH)

ZODIAC SIGNS —

English	Spanish	Pronounced
Aries	Aries	(AH-RIH-YEHS)
Taurus	Tauro	(TAH-OOH-ROH)
Gemini	Geminis	(HEH-MIH-NIHS)
Cancer	Cancer	(KAHN-SEHR)
Leo	Leo	(LEH-YOH)
Virgo	Virgo	(VIHR-GOH)
Libra	Libra	(LIH-BRAH)
Scorpio	Escorpion	(EHS-KOHR-PIH-YOHN)
Sagittarius	Sagitario	(SAH-HIH-TAH-RIH-YOH)
Capricorn	Capricornio	(KAH-PRIH-KOHR-NIH-YOH)
Aquarius	Acuario	(AH-KWAH-RIH-YOH)
Pisces	Piscis	(PIH-SIHS)

CHAPTER 3

Phrases

— BODY SEARCH

English	Spanish	Pronounced
This is a body search.	Esto es un registro de tu cuerpo.	(EHS-TOH) (EHS) (OOHN) (REH-HIHS-TROH) (DEH) (TOOH) (KWEHR-POH.)
Disrobe.	Desnudate.	(DEHS-NOOH-DAH-TEH.)
Take off all of your clothes.	Quitate toda tu ropa.	(KIH-TAH-TEH) (TOH-DAH) (TOOH) (ROH-PAH.)
The jewelry too.	Las joyas tambien.	(LAHS) (HOH-YAHS) (TAHM-BIH-YEHN.)
Run your fingers through your hair.	Corre los dedos sobre tu pelo.	(KOH-RREH) (LOHS) (DEH-DOHS) (SOH-BREH) (TOOH) (PEH-LOH.)
Show me the palms of your hands.	Enséñame las palmas de tus manos.	(EHN-SEH-NYAH-MEH) (LAHS) (PAHL-MAHS) (DEH) (TOOHS) (MAH-NOHS.)
Show me the bottoms of your feet.	Enséñame las plantas de tus pies.	(EHN-SEH-NYAH-MEH) (LAHS) (PLAHN-TAHS) (DEH) (TOOHS) (PIH-YEHS.)
If you are wearing a tampon, remove it.	Si tienes un tampon, quitate lo.	(SIH) (TIH-YIH-NEHS) (OOHN) (TAHM-POHN,) (KIH-TAH-TEH) (LOH.)

BODY SEARCH ——

English	Spanish	Pronounced
Bend over.	Agachese.	(AH-GAH-CHEH-SEH.)
Spread your buttocks with your hands.	Separe sus nalgas con sus manos.	(SEH-PAH-REH) (SOOHS) (NAHL-GAHS) (KOHN) (SOOHS) (MAH-NOHS.)
Don't move.	No te muevas.	(NOH) (TEH) (MWEH-VAHS.)
Get dressed.	Vistete.	(VIHS-TEH-TEH.)
Come with me.	Ven con migo.	(VEHN) (KOHN) (MIH-GOH.)
Go there.	Ve alla.	(VEH) (AH-YAH.)

Phrases

English	Spanish	Pronounced
The phone is there.	El telefono esta alli.	(EHL) (TEH-LEH-FOH-NOH) (EHS-TAH) (AH-YIH).
You're allowed one/two calls	Se le permite una/dos llamadas.	(SEH) (LEH) (PEHR-MIH-TEH) (OOH-NAH/DOHS) (YAH-MAH-DAHS).
The phone number here is	El numero de aqui es	(EHL) (NOOH-MEH-ROH) (DEH) (AH-KIH) (EHS...)
Place all your things here.	Ponga todas sus cosas aqui.	(POHN-GAH) (TOH-DAHS) (SOOHS) (KOH-SAHS) (AH-KIH).
They will be returned when you are released.	Seran regresado cuando quedes libre.	(SEH-RAHN) (REH-GREH-SAH-DOH) (KWAHN-DOH) (KEH-DEHS) (LIH-BREH).
Your car is there.	Tu carro esta alli.	(TOOH) (KAH-RROH) (EHS-TAH) (AH-YIH).
Are you ill?	¿Estas enfermo?	¿(EHS-TAHS) (EHN-FEHR-MOH)?
Are you in this country legally?	¿Estas en este paiz legalmente?	¿(EHS-TAHS) (EHN) (EHS-TEH) (PAH-YIHS) (LEH-GAHL-MEHN-TEH)?
Do you have identification?	¿Tienes identificacion?	¿(TIH-YEH-NEHS) (IH-DEHN-TIH-FIH-KAH-SYOHN)?

BOOKINGS ——

English	Spanish	Pronounced
Do you use any other name?	¿Usas algun otro nombre?	¿(OOH-SAHS) (AHL-GOOHN) (OH-TROH) (NOHM-BREH)?
Have you been arrested before?	¿A sido arrestado antes?	¿(AH) (SIH-DOH) (AH-RREHS-TAH-DOH) (AHN-TEHS)?
Go over there.	Ve para alla.	(VEH) (PAH-RAH) (AH-YAH).
Come here.	Ven aqui.	(VEHN) (AH-KIH).
I am going to take your fingerprints.	Voy a tomar tus huellas digitales.	(VOHY) (AH) (TOH-MAHR) (TOOHS) (HWEH-YAHS) (DIH-HIH-TAH-LES).
Clean your hands.	Limpiate las manos.	(LIHM-PIH-YAH-TEH) (LAHS) (MAH-NOHS).
I am going to take your picture.	Voy a tomar tu retrato.	(VOHY) (AH) (TOH-MAHR) (TOOH) (REH-TRAH-TOH).
Write it.	Escribelo.	(EHS-KRIH-BEH-LOH).
What is your name?	¿Como te llamas?	¿(KOH-MOH) (TEH) (YAH-MAHS)?
Where do you live?	¿Donde vives?	¿(DOHN-DEH) (VIH-VEHS)?

Phrases

— BOOKINGS

English	Spanish	Pronounced
What is your phone number?	¿Que es tu numero de telefono?	¿(KEH) (EHS) (TOOH) (NOOH-MEH-ROH) (DEH) (TEH-LEH-FOH-NOH)?
How old are you?	¿Cuantos anos tienes?	¿(KWAHN-TOS) (AH-NYOHS) (TIH-YEH-NEHS)?
What is your date of birth?	¿Que es tu fecha de nacimiento?	¿(KEH) (EHS) (TOOH) (FEH-CHAH) (DEH) (NAH-SIH-MIH-YEHN-TOH)?
What is your Social Security Number?	¿Que es tu Numero de Seguro Social?	¿(KEH) (EHS) (TOOH) (NOOH-MEH-ROH) (DEH) (SEH-GOOH-ROH) (SOH-SIH-YAHL)?
What is your occupation?	¿Que es tu trabajo?	¿(KEH) (EHS) (TOOH) (TRAH-BAH-HOH)?

BURGLARY/THEFT ——

English	Spanish	Pronounced
Do you know the brand?	¿Sabe la marca?	¿(SAH-BEH) (LAH) (MAHR-KAH)?
Do you know the serial number?	¿Sabe el numero de serie?	¿(SAH-BEH) (EHL) (NOOH-MEH-ROH) (DEH) (SEH-RIH-YEH)?
Was there a witness?	¿Hubo algun testigo?	¿(OOH-BOH) (AHL-GOOHN) (TEHS-TIH-GOH)?
Do you have any idea who did this?	¿Tiene alguna idea quien fue?	¿(TIH-YEH-NEH) (AHL-GOOHN-NAH) (IH-DEH-YAH) (KIH-YEHN) (FWEH)?
What was the license plate number?	¿Que es el numero de la placa?	¿(KEH) (EHS) (EHL) (NOOH-MEH-ROOH) (DEH) (LAH) (PLAH-KAH)?
What make?	¿Que marca?	¿(KEH) (MAHR-KAH)?
What year?	¿Que año?	¿(KEH) (AH-NYOH)?
What color?	¿Que color?	¿(KEH) (KOH-LOHR)?
Were you behind on your payments?	¿Estaba atrasado en sus pagos?	¿(EHS-TAH-BAH) (AH-TRAH-SAH-DOH) (EHN) (SOOHS) (PAH-GOHS)?

CHAPTER 3 **Phrases**

English	Spanish	Pronounced
Your conduct is against the law.	Su conducta es contra la ley.	(SOOH) (KOHN-DOOHK-TAH) (EHS) (KOHN-TRAH) (LAH) (LAY).
Leave!	¡Vayanse!	(VAH-YAHN-SEH)!
Do not come forward!	¡No se acercen!	(NOH) (SEH) (AH-SEHR-KEHN)!
Stay behind the barricades!	¡Quedense atras de la barrera!	(KEH-DEHN-SEH) (AH-TRAHS) (DEH) (LAH) (BAH-RREH-RAH)!
Leave now or be arrested.	Vayanse ahorita o seran arrestados.	(VAH-YAHN-SEH) (AH-OH-RIH-TAH) (OH) (SEH-RAHN) (AH-RREHS-TAH-DOHS).
Don't move!	¡No se muevan!	(NOH) (SEH) (MWEH-VAHN)!

DIRECTIVES ——

English	Spanish	Pronounced
Release the gun.	Suelta la pistola.	(SWEHL-TAH LAH PIHS-TOH-LAH).
Release the knife.	Suelta el cuchillo.	(SWEHL-TAH EHL KOOH-CHIH-YOH).
Release that.	Suelta eso.	(SWEHL-TAH EH-SOH).
Be quiet!	¡Callate!	(KAH-YAH-TEH)!
Calm yourself.	Calmese.	(KAHL-MEH-SEH).
Come with me.	Venga con migo.	(VEHN-GAH) (KOHN) (MIH-GOH).
Don't move.	No te muevas.	(NOH) (TEH) (MWEH-VAHS).
Keep walking.	Sige caminando.	(SIH-GEH) (KAH-MIH-NAHN-DOH).
Get in.	Metete.	(MEH-TEH-TEH).
Leave that.	Deja eso.	(DEH-HAH) (EH-SOH).
Get out of there.	Salte de alli.	(SAHL-TEH) (DEH) (AH-YIH).
Hands up.	Manos arriba.	(MAH-NOHS) (AH-RRIH-BAH).

Phrases

— DIRECTIVES

English	Spanish	Pronounced
I don't understand.	Yo no te entiendo.	(YOH) (NOH) (TEH) (EHN-TIH-YEHN-DOH).
I speak a little.	Yo hablo un poco.	(YOH) (AH-BLOH) (OOHN) (POH-KOH).
Kneel down.	Hincate.	(IHN-KAH-TEH).
Lie down.	Acuestate.	(AH-KWEHS-TAH-TEH).
Loosen your grip.	Suelta tu agarro.	(SWEHL-TAH) (TOOH) (AH-GAH-RROH).
Move your tongue.	Mueve tu lengua.	(MWEH-VEH) (TOOH) (LEHN-GWAH).
Open your mouth.	Abre tu boca.	(AH-BREH) (TOOH) (BOH-KAH).
Quickly.	Pronto.	(PROHN-TOH).
Show me proof of insurance.	Enseñame prueba de aseguranza/seguro.	(EHN-SEH-NYAH-MEH) (PROOH-WEH-BAH) (DEH) (AH-SEH-GOOH-RAHN-SAH/SEH-GOOH-ROH).
Show me your hands.	Enseñame tus manos.	(EHN-SEH-NYAH-MEH) (TOOHS) (MAH-NOHS).

DIRECTIVES ——

English	Spanish	Pronounced
Sign here.	Firme aqui.	(FIHR-MEH) (AH-KIH).
Sit down.	Sientate.	(SIH-YEHN-TAH-TEH).
Clean your hands.	Limpiate las manos.	(LIHM-PIH-YAH-TEH) (LAHS) (MAH-NOHS).
Slowly.	Despacio.	(DEHS-PAH-SYOH).
Spread your feet.	Abre los pies.	(AH-BREH) (LOHS) (PIH-YEHS).
Stand here.	Parate aqui.	(PAH-RAH-TEH) (AH-KIH).
Stand up.	Parate.	(PAH-RAH-TEH).
Stop.	Alto / Parate.	(AHL-TOH) / (PAH-RAH-TEH).
Don't touch.	No toques.	(NOH) (TOH-KEHS).
Take off your shoes.	Quitate tus zapatos.	(KIH-TAH-TEH) (TOOHS) (SAH-PAH-TOHS).
Take your hands out.	Saca tus manos.	(SAH-KAH) (TOOHS) (MAH-NOHS).

— DIRECTIVES

English	Spanish	Pronounced
Talk to me.	Habla con migo.	(AH-BLAH) (KOHN) (MIH-GOH).
Tell me in other words.	Dime con otras palabras.	(DIH-MEH) (KOHN) (OH-TRAHS) (PAH-LAH-BRAHS).
This is the case number.	Este es el numero del reporte.	(EHS-TEH) (EHS) (EHL) (NOOH-MEH-ROH) (DEHL) (REH-POHR-TEH).
Turn around.	Volteate.	(VOHL-TEH-YAH-TEH).
Turn off the engine.	Apaga el motor.	(AH-PAH-GAH) (EHL) (MOH-TOHR).
You are under arrest.	Estas arrestado.	(EHS-TAHS) (AH-RREHS-TAH-DOH).
Wake up.	Dispiertate.	(DIHS-PIH-YEHR-TAH-TEH).
Write it.	Escribelo.	(EHS-KRIH-BEH-LOH).

DOMESTIC DISTURBANCES ——

English	Spanish	Pronounced
Calm down.	Calmese.	(KAHL-MEH-SEH).
Who called?	¿Quien llamo?	¿(KIH-YEHN) (YAH-MOH)?
What is your name?	¿Como te llamas?	¿(KOH-MOH) (TEH) (YAH-MAHS)?
What is your date of birth?	¿Que es tu fecha de nacimiento?	¿(KEH) (EHS) (TOOH) (FEH-CHAH) (DEH) (NAH-SIH-MYEHN-TOH)?
Do you live here?	¿Vives aqui?	¿(VIH-VEHS) (AH-KIH)?
Where do you live?	¿Donde vives?	¿(DOHN-DEH) (VIH-VEHS)?
Are you hurt?	¿Estas lastimado?	¿(EHS-TAHS) (LAHS-TIH-MAH-DOH)?
Did he hit you?	¿Te pego?	¿(TEH) (PEH-GOH)?
Let's talk over there.	Vamos hablar alla.	(VAH-MOHS) (AH-BLAHR) (AH-YAH).

Phrases

— DOMESTIC DISTURBANCES

English	Spanish	Pronounced
Is he armed?	¿Esta armado?	¿(EHS-TAH) (AHR-MAH-DOH)?
Is he your husband?	¿Es tu esposo?	¿(EHS) (TOOH) (EHS-POH-SOH)?
Where are the children?	¿Donde estan los niños?	¿(DOHN-DEH) (EHS-TAHN) (LOHS) (NIH-NYOHS)?
Do you want to file charges?	¿Quiere ponerle cargos?	¿(KIH-YEH-REH) (POH-NEHR-LEH) (KAHR-GOHS)?
Do you want to go to the women's shelter?	¿Quiere ir al refugio de mujeres?	¿(KIH-YEH-REH) (IHR) (AHL) (REH-FOOH-HYOH) (DEH) (MOOH-HEH-REHS)?
Bring only your personal clothing.	Traiga su ropa personal.	(TRAH-IH-GAH) (SOOH) (ROH-PAH) (PEHR-SOH-NAHL)

DWI —

English	Spanish	Pronounced
You were driving badly.	Usted estaba manejando mal.	(OOHS-TEHD) (EHS-TAH-BAH) (MAH-NEH-HAHN-DOH) (MAHL).
Have you been drinking alcohol?	¿A estado bebiendo alcohol?	¿(AH) (EHS-TAH-DOH) (BEH-BIH-YEHN-DOH) (AHL-KOHL).
Have you taken any drugs?	¿A tomado alguna droga?	¿(AH) (TOH-MAH-DOH) (AHL-GOOH-NAH) (DROH-GAH).
Step out of the car.	Salga del carro.	(SAHL-GAH) (DEHL) (KAH-RROH).
I am going to test you to see if you are intoxicated.	Le voy a dar unas pruebas para ver si estad intoxicado.	(LEH) (VOHY) (AH) (DAHR) (OOH-NAHS) (PROOH-WEH-BAHS) (PAH-RAH) (VEHR) (SIH) (EHS-TAHD) (IHN-TOHK-SIH-KAH-DOH).
See DWI - Field Sobriety Tests. Be sure to document any / all details observed during the tests.		
You did not cooperate, so you are under arrest.	Usted no coopero solo que estas arrestado.	(OOHS-TEHD) (NOH) (KOH-OH-PEH-ROH) (SOH-LOH) (KEH) (EHS-TAHS) (AH-RREHS-TAH-DOH).

Phrases

— DWI

English	Spanish	Pronounced
You did not pass the tests.	Usted no paso las pruebas.	(OOHS-TEHD) (NOH) (PAH-SOH) (LAHS) (PROOH-WEH-BAHS).
You are under arrest for driving while intoxicated.	Usted estad arrestado por manejar intoxicado.	(OOHS-TEHD) (EHS-TAHD) (AH-RREHS-TAH-DOH) (POHR) (MAH-NEH-HAHR) (IHN-TOHK-SIH-KAH-DOH).
I ask that you submit to a test of your breath/ blood,	Yo le pido que someta una prueba de su aliento/ sangre,	(YOH) (LEH) (PIH-DOH) (KEH) (SOH-MEH-TAH) (OOH-NAH) (PROOH-WEH-BAH) (DEH) (SOOH) (AH-LIH-YEHN-TOH) / (SAHN-GREH),
to determine the content of alcohol in your blood.	para determinar el contenido de alcohol en su sangre.	(PAH-RAH) (DEH-TEHR-MIH-NAHR) (EHL) (KOHN-TEH-NIH-DOH) (DEH) (AHL-KOHL) (EHN) (SOOH) (SAHN-GREH).
If you refuse this test, your license will be suspended.	Si se niega a esta prueba, su licensia sera suspendida.	(SIH) (SEH) (NIH-YEH-GAH) (AH) (EHS-TAH) (PROOH-WEH-BAH,) (SOOH) (LIH-SEHN-SIH-YAH) (SEH-RAH) (SOOHS-PEHN-DIH-DAH).

DWI —

English	Spanish	Pronounced
The test indicates that you have had more than the legal limit of alcohol in your blood.	La prueba indica que usted tiene mas de el limite legal de alcohol en su sangre.	(LAH) (PROOH-WEH-BAH) (IHN-DIH-KAH) (KEH) (OOHS-TEHD) (TIH-YEH-NEH) (MAHS) (DEH) (EHL) (LIH-MIH-TEH) (LEH-GAHL) (DEH) (AHL-KOHL) (EHN) (SOOH) (SAHN-GREH).
You passed the test.	Usted paso la prueba.	(OOHS-TEHD) (PAH-SOH) (LAH) (PROOH-WEH-BAH).
You are free to go.	Usted queda libre.	(OOHS-TEHD) (KEH-DAH) (LIH-BREH).
You car will be returned to you.	Su carro sera regresado a usted.	(SOOH) (KAH-RROH) (SEH-RAH) (REH-GREH-SAH-DOH) (AH) (OOHS-TEHD).

Phrases

— DWI, FIELD SOBRIETY
ROMBURG BALANCE TEST

English	Spanish	Pronounced
Please do exactly as I say, and begin only when I tell you to.	Por favor haga exactamente lo que yo le digo, y comiense nomas cuando yo le digo.	(POHR) (FAH-VOHR) (AH-GAH) (EHK-SAHK-TAH-MEHN-TEH) (LOH) (KEH) (YOH) (LEH) (DIH-GOH) (EE) (KOH-MIH-YEHN-SEH) (NOH-MAHS) (KWAHN-DOH) (YOH) (LEH) (DIH-GOH).
1. Close your eyes.	1. Cierre los ojos.	(SIH-YEH-RREH) (LOHS) (OH-HOHS).
2. Tilt your head all the way back.	2. Ladea la cabeza para atras totalmente.	(LAH-DEH-YAH) (LAH) (KAH-BEH-SAH) (PAH-RAH) (AH-TRAHS) (TOH-TAHL-MEHN-TEH)
3. Calculate thirty seconds.	3. Calcule treinta segundos.	(KAHL-KOOH-LEH) (TREH-IHN-TAH) (SEH-GOOHN-DOHS).
4. At the end, straighten yourself	4. A su fin enderezate.	(AH) (SOOH) (FIHN) (EHN-DEH-REH-SAH-TEH).
5. Open your eyes.	5. Abre tus ojos.	(AH-BREH) (TOOHS) (OH-HOHS).

DWI, FIELD SOBRIETY
ROMBURG BALANCE TEST ——

English	Spanish	Pronounced
You must figure out the time, I will not help you.	Tu figuraras el tiempo, yo no te ayudare.	(TOOH) (FIH-GOOH-RAH-RAHS) (EHL) (TIH-YEHM-POH,) (YOH) (NOH) (TEH) (AH-YOOH-DAH-REH).
Do you understand?	¿Entiendes?	¿(EHN-TIH-YEHN-DEHS)?
[yes or no]	[si o no]	[(SIH) (OH) (NOH)]
Begin.	Comiense.	(KOH-MIH-YEHN-SEH).

Phrases

— DWI, FIELD SOBRIETY
NOSE TOUCH TEST

English	Spanish	Pronounced
Please do exactly as I say, and begin only when I tell you to.	Por favor haga exactamente lo que yo le digo, y comiense nomas cuando yo le digo.	(POHR) (FAH-VOHR) (AH-GAH) (EHK-SAHK-TAH-MEHN-TEH) (LOH) (KEH) (YOH) (LEH) (DIH-GOH) (EE) (KOH-MIH-YEHN-SEH) (NOH-MAHS) (KWAHN-DOH) (YOH) (LEH) (DIH-GOH).
1. Keep your hands at your sides.	1. Ponga sus manos a su lado.	(POHN-GAH) (SOOHS) (MAH-NOHS) (AH) (SOOH) (LAH-DOH).
2. Put the palms of your hands toward me.	2. Ponga sus manos palma arriba.	(POHN-GAH) (SOOHS) (MAH-NOHS) (PAHL-MAH) (AH-RRIH-BAH).
3. Close your hands.	3. Cierre sus manos.	(SIH-YEH-RREH) (SOOHS) (MAH-NOHS).
4. Point down with your index fingers.	4. Apunte con sus dedos primeros hacia abajo.	(AH-POOHN-TEH) (KOHN) (SOOHS) (DEH-DOHS) (PRIH-MEH-ROHS) (AH-SIH-YAH) (AH-BAH-HOH).
5. With your index finger touch the tip of your nose.	5. Toquese la nariz con su dedo.	(TOH-KEH-SEH) (LAH) (NAH-RIHS) (KOHN) (SOOH) (DEH-DOH).

DWI, FIELD SOBRIETY
NOSE TOUCH TEST —

English	Spanish	Pronounced
6. Bring your hand down.	6. Baje la mano.	(BAH-HEH) (LAH) (MAH-NOH).
7. I will tell you which finger to use.	7. Yo le dire cual dedo que use.	(YOH) (LEH) (DIH-REH) (KWAHL) (DEH-DOH) (KEH) (OOH-SEH).
8. Close your eyes.	8. Cierre los ojos.	(SIH-YEH-RREH) (LOHS) (OH-HOHS).
9. Tilt your head all the way back.	9. Ladea la cabeza para atras totalmente.	(LAH-DEH-YAH) (LAH) (KAH-BEH-SAH) (PAH-RAH) (AH-TRAHS) (TOH-TAHL-MEHN-TEH).
Do you understand?	¿Entiendes?	(EHN-TIH-YEHN-DEHS)?
[yes or no]	[si o no]	[(SIH) (OH) (NOH)]
Begin with:	Comiense con:	(KOH-MIH-YEHN-SEH) (KOHN:)
(1) your left finger	(1) su dedo izquierdo	(SOOH) (DEH-DOH) (IHS-KIH-YEHR-DOH)
(2) your right finger	(2) su dedo derecho	(SOOH) (DEH-DOH) (DEH-REH-CHOH)

Phrases

— DWI, FIELD SOBRIETY NOSE TOUCH TEST

English	Spanish	Pronounced
(3) your left finger	(3) su dedo izquierdo	(SOOH) (DEH-DOH) (IHS-KIH-YEHR-DOH)
(4) your left finger	(4) su dedo izquierdo	(SOOH) (DEH-DOH) (IHS-KIH-YEHR-DOH)
(5) your right finger	(5) su dedo derecho	(SOOH) (DEH-DOH) (DEH-REH-CHOH)
(6) your left finger	(6) su dedo izquierdo	(SOOH) (DEH-DOH) (IHS-KIH-YEHR-DOH)
#3 and #4 are purposely repeated.		

DWI, FIELD SOBRIETY
ONE LEG STAND TEST ——

English	Spanish	Pronounced
Please do exactly as I say, and begin only when I tell you to.	Por favor haga exactamente lo que yo le digo, y comiense nomas cuando yo le digo.	(POHR) (FAH-VOHR) (AH-GAH) (EHK-SAHK-TAH-MEHN-TEH) (LOH) (KEH) (YOH) (LEH) (DIH-GOH) (EE) (KOH-MIH-YEHN-SEH) (NOH-MAHS) (KWAHN-DOH) (YOH) (LEH) (DIH-GOH).
1. Stand with your heels together.	1. Ponga los tobillos juntos.	(POHN-GAH) (LOHS) (TOH-BIH-YOHS) (HOOHN-TOHS).
2. Put your hands at your sides.	2. Deje las manos a su lado.	(DEH-HEH) (LAHS) (MAH-NOHS) (AH) (SOOH) (LAH-DOH).
3. Raise one leg six inches from the ground.	3. Suba un pie a seiz pulgadas del suelo.	(SOOH-BAH) (OOHN) (PIH-YEH) (AH) (SAYS) (POOHL-GAH-DAHS) (DEHL) (SWEH-LOH).
4. Hold it stiff there.	4. Detengalo duro.	(DEH-TEHN-GAH-LOH) (DOOH-ROH).
5. Count out loud from 1001 to 1030.	5. Cuente, a voz alta, de mil y uno a mil y treinta.	(KWEHN-TEH) (AH) (VOHS) (AHL-TAH) (DEH) (MIHL) (EE) (OOH-NOH) (AH) (MIHL) (EE) (TREH-IHN-TAH).

— DWI, FIELD SOBRIETY
ONE LEG STAND TEST

English	Spanish	Pronounced
6. Do it first with your left leg,	6. Hagalo primero con su pie izquierdo,	(AH-GAH-LOH) (PRIH-MEH-ROH) (KOHN) (SOOH) (PIH-YEH) (IHS-KIH-YEHR-DOH).
7. Then with your right leg.	7. Despues con su pie derecho.	(DEHS-PWEHS) (KOHN) (SOOH) (PIH-YEH) (DEH-REH-CHOH).
Once you start, do not stop until finished.	Al comensar, no pare hasta acabar.	(AHL) (KOH-MEHN-SAHR) (NOH) (PAH-REH) (AHS-TAH) (AH-KAH-BAHR).
Do you understand?	¿Entiendes?	¿(EHN-TIH-YEHN-DEHS)?
[yes or no]	[si o no]	[(SIH) (OH) (NOH)]
Begin.	Comiense.	(KOH-MIH-YEHN-SEH).

DWI, FIELD SOBRIETY
WALKING TEST ——

English	Spanish	Pronounced
Please do exactly as I say, and begin only when I tell you to.	Por favor haga exactamente lo que yo le digo, y comiense nomas cuando yo le digo.	(POHR) (FAH-VOHR) (AH-GAH) (EHK-SAHK-TAH-MEHN-TEH) (LOH) (KEH) (YOH) (LEH) (DIH-GOH) (EE) (KOH-MIH-YEHN-SEH) (NOH-MAHS) (KWAHN-DOH) (YOH) (LEH) (DIH-GOH).
1. Put your right foot here.	1. Ponga el pie derecho aqui.	(POHN-GAH) (EHL) (PIH-YEH) (DEH-REH-CHOH) (AH-KIH).
2. Put your left foot in front of it.	2. Ponga el pie izquierdo en frente de el.	(POHN-GAH) (EHL) (PIH-YEH) (IHS-KIH-YEHR-DOH) (EHN) (FREHN-TEH) (DEH) (EHL).
3. They must be heel-to-toe.	3. Tienen que estar tobillo-a-punta.	(TIH-YEH-NEHN) (KEH) (EHS-TAHR) (TOH-BIH-YOH) (AH) (POOHN-TAH).
4. Keep your hands at your sides.	4. Deje las manos a su lado.	(DEH-HEH) (LAHS) (MAH-NOHS) (AH) (SOOH) (LAH-DOH).

126

Phrases

— DWI, FIELD SOBRIETY
WALKING TEST

English	Spanish	Pronounced
5. When I say, take ten heel-to-toe steps.	5. Cuando yo diga tome diez pasos de tobillo-a-punta.	(KWAHN-DOH) (YOH) (DIH-GAH) (TOH-MEH) (DIH-YEHS) (PAH-SOHS) (DEH) (TOH-BIH-YOH) (AH) (POOHN-TAH).
6. Watch your feet.	6. Observa sus pies.	(OHB-SEHR-VAH) (SOOHS) (PIH-YEHS).
7. Count each step out loud.	7. Cuente cada paso en voz alta.	(KWEHN-TEH) (KAH-DAH) (PAH-SOH) (EHN) (VOHS) (AHL-TAH).
Once you start, do not stop until finished.	Al comensar, no pare hasta acabar.	(AHL) (KOH-MEHN-SAHR) (NOH) (PAH-REH) (AHS-TAH) (AH-KAH-BAHR).
Do you understand?	¿Entiendes?	¿(EHN-TIH-YEHN-DEHS)?
[yes or no]	[si o no]	[(SIH) (OH) (NOH)]
Begin.	Comiense.	(KOH-MIH-YEHN-SEH).

FELONY CAR STOP ——

English	Spanish	Pronounced
driver	chófer	(CHOH-FEHR)
passenger	pasajero	(PAH-SAH-HEH-ROH)
don't move	no te muevas	(NOH) (TEH) (MWEH-VAHS)
turn off the motor	apaga el motor	(AH-PAH-GAH) (EHL) (MOH-TOHR)
put your hands on the window	ponga las manos en la ventana	(POHN-GAH) (LAHS) (MAH-NOHS) (EHN) (LAH) (VEHN-TAH-NAH)
you, in the back seat	tu, en el asiento de atras,	(TOOH,) (EHN) (EHL) (AH-SIH-YEHN-TOH) (DEH) (AH-TRAHS)
put your hands on the back of the seat	ponga las manos en el respaldar del asiento	(POHN-GAH) (LAHS) (MAH-NOHS) (EHN) (EHL) (REHS-PAHL-DAHR) (DEHL) (AH-SIH-YEHN-TOH).
open the window	abre la ventana	(AH-BREH) (LAH) (VEHN-TAH-NAH)
throw the keys out	tire las llaves fuera	(TIH-REH) (LAHS) (YAH-VEHS) (FWEH-RAH)

Phrases

— FELONY CAR STOP

English	Spanish	Pronounced
reach out and open the door from the outside	saque sus manos y abra la puerta por fuera	(SAH-KEH) (SOOHS) (MAH-NOHS) (EE) (AH-BRAH) (LAH) (PWEHR-TAH) (POHR) (FWEH-RAH)
get out, slowly	salga, despacio	(SAHL-GAH), (DEHS-PAH-SIH-YOH)
turn around	volteate	(VOHL-TEH-YAH-TEH)
give me your back	dame tu espalda	(DAH-MEH) (TOOH) (EHS-PAHL-DAH)
walk to me	camina hacia mi	(KAH-MIH-NAH) (AH-SIH-YAH) (MIH)
stop	alto	(AHL-TOH)
kneel	hincate	(IHN-KAH-TEH)
lay down, face down	acuestate, bocabajo	(AH-KWEHS-TAH-TEH,) (BOH-KAH-BAH-HOH)

FOUND PERSON ——

English	Spanish	Pronounced
What is your name?	¿Como te llamas?	¿(KOH-MOH) (TEH) (YAH-MAHS)?
How old are you?	¿Cuantos años tienes?	¿(KWAHN-TOHS) (AH-NYOHS) (TIH-YEH-NEHS)?
Where do you live?	¿Donde vives?	¿(DOHN-DEH) (VIH-VEHS)?
What is your phone number?	¿Que es tu numero de telefono?	¿(KEH) (EHS) (TOOH) (NOOH-MEH-ROH) (DEH) (TEH-LEH-FOH-NOH)?
Is your family coming?	¿Viene tu familia?	¿(VIH-YEH-NEH) (TOOH) (FAH-MIH-LIH-YAH)?
Did you go with a stranger?	¿Te fuiste con un desconocido?	¿(TEH) (FOOH-WIHS-TEH) (KOHN) (OOHN) (DEHS-KOH-NOH-SIH-DOH)?
Come with me.	Ven conmigo.	(VEHN) (KOHN-MIH-GOH)
I will help you.	Yo te ayudare.	(YOH) (TEH) (AH-YOOH-DAH-REH)

— LINEUPS/SUSPECTS

English	Spanish	Pronounced
You match the description of a suspect.	Usted queda a la descripcion de un suspechoso.	(OOHS-TEHD) (KEH-DAH) (AH) (LAH) (DEHS-KRIHP-SIH-YOHN) (DEH) (OOHN) (SOHS-PEH-CHOH-SOH)
You are detained for identification.	Usted esta detenido para identificacion	(OOHS-TEHD) (EHS-TAH) (DEH-TEH-NIH-DOH) (PAH-RAH) (IH-DEHN-TIH-FIH-KAH-SIH-YOHN)
You do not have the right to refuse.	Usted no tiene el derecho de negarse	(OOHS-TEHD) (NOH) (TIH-YEH-NEH) (EHL) (DEH-REH-CHOH) (DEH) (NEH-GAHR-SEH)
If you refuse, it can and will be used against you in court.	Si se niega, se puede y sera usado contra usted en corte	(SIH) (SEH) (NIH-YEH-GAH,) (SEH) (POOH-WEH-DEH) (EE) (SEH-RAH) (OOH-SAH-DOH) (KOHN-TRAH) (OOHS-TEHD) (EHN) (KOHR-TEH)
This group of people / photos possibly contains the person who committed the crime.	Este grupo de gente / fotos posiblemente contiene la persona responsable por el crimen	(EHS-TEH) (GROOH-POH) (DEH) (HEHN-TEH) / (FOH-TOHS) (POH-SIH-BLEH-MEHN-TEH) (KOHN-TIH-YEH-NEH) (LAH) (PEHR-SOH-NAH) (REHS-POHN-SAH-BLEH) (POHR) (EHL) (KRIH-MEHN)

LINEUPS/SUSPECTS ——

English	Spanish	Pronounced
Make an identification only if you are reasonably sure of it.	Haga su identificacion solamente si estad razonablemente seguro.	(AH-GAH) (SOOH) (IH-DEHN-TIH-FIH-KAH-SIH-YOHN) (SOH-LAH-MEHN-TEH) (SIH) (EHS) (TAHD) (RAH-SOH-NAH-BLEH-MEHN-TEH) (SEH-GOOH-ROH)
You are not obligated to make any identification.	Usted no esta obligado de hacer una identificacion.	(OOHS-TEHD) (NOH) (EHS-TAH) (OHB-LIH-GAH-DOH) (DEH) (AH-SEHR) (OOH-NAH) (IH-DEHN-TIH-FIH-KAH-SIH-YOHN)
Thank you.	Muchas gracias.	(MOOH-CHAS) (GRAH-SIH-YAHS)

Phrases

— MEDICAL

English	Spanish	Pronounced
Calm down.	Calmese.	(KAHL-MEH-SEH)
Everything will be alright.	Todo estara bien.	(TOH-DOH) (EHS-TAH-RAH) (BIH-YEHN)
The ambulance is coming.	La ambulancia ya viene.	(LAH) (AHM-BOOH-LAHN-SIH-YAH) (YAH) (VIH-YEH-NEH)
Are you sick?	¿Estas enfermo?	¿(EHS-TAHS) (EHN-FEHR-MOH)?
Do you have AIDS?	¿Tienes SIDA?	¿(TIH-YEH-NEHS) (SIH-DAH)?
Can you breathe?	¿Puedes respirar?	¿(PWEH-DEHS)(REHS-PIH-RAHR)?
Do you have pain?	¿Tienes dolor?	¿(TIH-YEH-NEHS) (DOH-LOHR)?
Where?	¿Donde?	¿(DOHN-DEH)?
Are you on medication?	¿Tomas alguna medicina?	¿(TOH-MAHS) (AHL-GOOH-NAH) (MEH-DIH-SIH-NAH)?
Do you have diabetes?	¿Tienes diabetis?	¿(TIH-YEH-NEHS) (DIH-YAH-BEH-TIHS)?

MEDICAL ——

English	Spanish	Pronounced
Are you pregnant?	¿Estas embarazada?	¿(EHS-TAHS) (EHM-BAH-RAH-SAH-DAH)?
Could it be only nerves?	¿No seran nervios solamente?	¿(NOH) (SEH-RAHN) (NEHR-VIH-YOHS) (SOH-LAH-MEHN-TEH)?
Were you raped?	¿Fue usted violada?	¿(FWEH) (OOHS-TEHD) (VIH-YOH-LAH-DAH)?
Did you take any drugs?	¿Tomaste alguna droga?	¿(TOH-MAHS-TEH) (AHL-GOOH-NAH) (DROH-GAH)?
Are you nauseated?	¿Tienes tu estomago revuelto?	¿(TIH-YEH-NEHS) (TOOH) (EHS-TOH-MAH-GOH) (REH-VOOH-WEHL-TOH)?
Are you dizzy?	¿Estas mareado?	¿(EHS-TAHS) (MAH-REH-YAH-DOH)?
Is it your heart?	¿Sera tu corazon?	¿(SEH-RAH) (TOOH) (KOH-RAH-SOHN)?
What is your blood type?	¿Que es tu tipo de sangre?	¿(KEH) (EHS) (TOOH) (TIH-POH) (DEH) (SAHN-GREH)?
Which hospital do you want to go to?	¿A cual hospital quieres ir?	¿(AH) (KWAHL) (OHS-PIH-TAHL) (KIH-YEH-REHS) (IHR)?

Phrases

— MEDICAL

English	Spanish	Pronounced
Where does it hurt?	¿Donde te duele?	¿(DOHN-DEH) (TEH) (DOOH-WEH-LEH)?
Can you feel your fingers/toes?	¿Sientes los dedos?	¿(SIH-YEHN-TES) (LOHS) (DEH-DOHS)?
Are you allergic to anything?	¿Eres alergico a algo?	¿(EH-REHS) (AH-LEHR-HIH-KOH) (AH) (AHL-GOH)?
What are you allergic to?	¿A que estas alergico?	¿(AH) (KEH) (EHS-TAHS) (AH-LEHR-HIH-KOH)?

MISSING PERSON ——

English	Spanish	Pronounced
What is his name?	¿Como se llama?	¿(KOH-MOH) (SEH) (YAH-MAH)?
When was he born?	¿Cuando nacio?	¿(KWAHN-DOH) (NAH-SIH-YOH)?
How tall?	¿Que tan alto?	¿(KEH) (TAHN) (AHL-TOH)?
How much does he weigh?	¿Cuanto pesa?	¿(KWAHN-TOH) (PEH-SAH)?
What color is his hair?	¿Que color es su pelo?	¿(KEH) (KOH-LOHR) (EHS) (SOOH) (PEH-LOH)?
Is it long or short?	¿Es largo o corto?	¿(EHS) (LAHR-GOH) (OH) (KOHR-TOH)?
Is it curly or straight?	¿Es rizado o lizo?	¿(EHS) (RIH-SAH-DOH) (OH) (LIH-SOH)?
What color are his eyes?	¿Que color son sus ojos?	¿(KEH) (KOH-LOHR) (SOHN) (SOOHS) (OH-HOHS)?
Does he have a mustache?	¿Tiene bigote?	¿(TIH-YEH-NEH) (BIH-GOH-TEH)?
...a beard?	¿Tiene barba?	¿(TIH-YEH-NEH) (BAHR-BAH)?

Phrases

— MISSING PERSON

English	Spanish	Pronounced
...any tatoos?	¿Tiene tatuajes?	¿(TIH-YEH-NEH)(TAH-TWAH-HEHS)?
...any scars?	¿Tiene cicatrizes?	¿(TIH-YEH-NEH) (SIH-KAH-TRIH-SEHS)?
What was he wearing?	¿Que tenia puesto?	¿(KEH) (TEH-NIH-YAH) (PWEHS-TOH)?
Pants Shirt Dress Skirt	pantalones camisa vestido falda	(PAHN-TAH-LOH-NEHS) (KAH-MIH-SAH) (VEHS-TIH-DOH) (FAHL-DAH)
What color?	¿De que color?	¿(DEH) (KEH) (KOH-LOHR)?
When was he last seen?	¿Cuando lo vieron por ultima vez?	¿(KWAHN-DOH) (LOH) (VIH-YEH-ROHN) (POHR) (OOHL-TIH-MAH) (VEHS)?
Where was he last seen?	¿Donde lo vieron por ultima vez?	¿(DOHN-DEH) (LOH) (VIH-YEH-ROHN) (POHR) (OOHL-TIH-MAH) (VEHS)?
Who last saw him?	¿Quien lo vio por ultima vez?	¿(KIH-YEHN) (LOH) (VIH-YOH) (POHR) (OOHL-TIH-MAH) (VEHS)?
Where was he going?	¿Para donde iva?	¿(PAH-RAH) (DOHN-DEH) (IH-VAH)?

MISSING PERSON —

English	Spanish	Pronounced
Was he going alone?	¿Iva solo?	¿(IH-VAH) (SOH-LOH)?
Have you searched at the school?	¿Han buscado en la escuela?	¿(AHN) (BOOHS-KAH-DOH) (EHN) (LAH) (EHS-KWEH-LAH)?
Have you searched at work?	¿Han buscado en el trabajo?	¿(AHN) (BOOHS-KAH-DOH) (EHN) (EHL) (TRAH-BAH-HOH)?
Have you searched at his family?	¿Han buscado con su familia?	¿(AHN) (BOOHS-KAH-DOH) (KOHN) (SOOH) (FAH-MIH-LIH-YAH)?
Have you searched at his friends?	¿Han buscado con sus amigos?	¿(AHN) (BOOHS-KAH-DOH) (KOHN) (SOOHS) (AH-MIH-GOHS)?
Has he recently been punished?	¿Ha sido castigado reciente?	¿(AH) (SIH-DOH) (KAHS-TIH-GAH-DOH) (REH-SIH-YEHN-TEH)?
Has he runaway before?	¿Se ha huido antes?	¿(SEH) (AH) (OOH-YIH-DOH) (AHN-TEHS)?
Do you have a photo?	¿Tienen una foto?	¿(TIH-YEH-NEHN) (OOH-NAH) (FOH-TOH)?

Phrases

— NOTIFICATIONS

English	Spanish	Pronounced
This is the police / sheriff department.	Este es el departamento de policia / sheriff.	(EHS-TEH) (EHS) (EHL) (DEH-PAHR-TAH-MEHN-TOH) (DEH) (POH-LIH-SIH-YAH) / (SHEH-RIHF)
[...] has been arrested for [...] (see section on crimes)	[...] ha sido arrestado por [...]	(...) (AH) (SIH-DOH) (AH-RREHS-TAH-DOH) (POHR...)
He can be released on bail.	Puede ser soltado bajo fianza.	(PWEH-DEH) (SEHR) (SOHL-TAH-DOH) (BAH-HOH) (FIH-YAHN-SAH)
He is held without bail.	Esta detendio sin fianza.	(EHS-TAH) (DEH-TEH-NIH-DOH) (SIHN) (FIH-YAHN-SAH)
The jail address is [...]	La direccion de la carcel es [...]	(LAH) (DIH-REHK-SIH-YOHN) (DEH) (LAH) (KAHR-SEHL) (EHS) (...)
The jail phone number is [...](see section on numbers)	El numero de telefono de la carcel es [...]	(EHL) (NOOH-MEH-ROH) (DEH) (TEH-LEH-FOH-NOH) (DEH) (LAH) (KAHR-SEHL) (EHS) (...)

QUESTIONS ——

English	Spanish	Pronounced
Speak English?	¿Hablas Ingles?	¿(AH-BLAHS) (IHN-GLEHS)?
What's your name?	¿Como te llamas?	¿(KOH-MOH) (TEH) (YAH-MAHS)?
Are you in danger?	¿Estas en peligro?	¿(EHS-TAHS) (EHN) (PEH-LIH-GROH)?
Where do you live?	¿Donde vives?	¿(DOHN-DEH) (VIH-VEHS)?
How old are you?	¿Cuantos años tienes?	¿(KWAHN-TOHS) (AHN-YOHS) (TIH-YEH-NEHS)?
Do you have children?	¿Tienes niños?	¿(TIH-YEH-NEHS) (NIH-NYOHS)?
Are you hurt?	¿Estas lastimado?	¿(EHS-TAHS) (LAHS-TIH-MAH-DOH)?
Are you married?	¿Eres casado?	¿(EH-REHS) (KAH-SAH-DOH)?
Do you want EMS?	¿Quieres una ambulancia?	¿(KIH-YEH-REHS) (OOH-NAH) (AHM-BOOH-LAHN-SIH-YAH)?
How many?	¿Cuantos?	¿(KWAHN-TOHS)?
Are they armed?	¿Estan armados?	¿(EHS-TAHN) (AHR-MAH-DOS)?

Phrases

— QUESTIONS

English	Spanish	Pronounced
How did they enter?	¿Como entraron?	¿(KOH-MOH) (EHN-TRAH-ROHN)?
What happened?	¿Que paso?	¿(KEH) (PAH-SOH)?
What is missing?	¿Que falta?	¿(KEH) (FAHL-TAH)?
Is it yours?	¿Es tuyo?	¿(EHS) (TOOH-YOH)?
How many beers?	¿Cuantas cervezas?	¿(KWAHN-TAHS) (SEHR-VEH-SAHS)?
Who is the owner?	¿Quien es el dueño?	¿(KIH-YEHN) (EHS) (EHL) (DWEH-NYOH)?
Where were you born?	¿Dondé naciste?	¿(DOHN-DEH) (NAH-SIHS-TEH)?
When were you born?	¿Cuando naciste?	¿(KWAHN-DOH) (NAH-SIHS-TEH)?
What is your telephone number?	¿Que es tu numero de telefono?	¿(KEH) (EHS) (TOOH) (NOOH-MEH-ROH) (DEH) (TEH-LEH-FOH-NOH)?
What is your address?	¿Que es tu direccion?	¿(KEH) (EHS) (TOOH) (DIH-REHK-SYOHN)?

QUESTIONS —

English	Spanish	Pronounced
What is your zip code?	¿Que es tu zona postal?	¿(KEH) (EHS) (TOOH) (SOH-NAH) (POHS-TAHL)?
What is your work address?	¿Que es tu direccion de trabajo?	¿(KEH) (EHS) (TOOH) (DIH-REHK-SYOHN) (DEH) (TRAH-BAH-HOH)?
Do you understand?	¿Me entendiste?	¿(MEH) (EHN-TEHN-DIHS-TEH)?

— TRAFFIC STOPS

English	Spanish	Pronounced
Turn off the motor.	Apague el motor.	(AH-PAH-GEH) (EHL) (MOH-TOR).
Step out of the car.	Salga del carro.	(SAHL-GAH) (DEHL) (KAH-RROH).
Return to your car.	Regrese a su carro.	(REH-GREH-SEH) (AH) (SOOH) (KAH-RROH).
Show me your Driver's License, please.	Enseñeme su liscensia, por favor.	(EHN-SEH-NYEH-MEH) (SOOH) (LIH-SEHN-SYAH) (POHR) (FAH-VOHR).
Take it out, please.	Saquela, por favor.	(SAH-KEH-LAH,) (POHR) (FAH-VOHR).
Show me proof of insurance, please.	Enseñeme prueba de seguro/asegura nza, por favor.	(EHN-SEH-NYEH-MEH) (PROOH-WEH-BAH) (DEH) (SEG-GOOH-ROH/AH-SEH-GOOH-RAHN-SAH,) (POHR) (FAH-VOHR).
Do you live here?	¿Vives aqui?	¿(VIH-VEHS) (AH-KIH)?
You did not use your seat belt.	Usted no uso su cinturon.	(OOHS-TEHD) (NOH) (OOH-SOH) (SOOH) (SIHN-TOOH-ROHN).

TRAFFIC STOPS —

English	Spanish	Pronounced
You were speeding.	Usted iba demasiado recio.	(OOHS-TEHD) (IH-BAH) (DEH-MAH-SYAH-DOH) (REH-SIH-YOH).
You passed a stop sign.	Usted se paso alto.	(OOHS-TEHD) (SEH) (PAH-SOH) (EHL) (AHL-TOH).
You passed the red light.	Usted se paso el zemaforo rojo / Usted se paso la luz colorada.	(OOHS-TEHD) (SEH) (PAH-SOH) (EHL) (SEH-MAH-FOH-ROH) (ROH-HOH). / (OOHS-TEHD) (SEH) (PAH-SOH) (LAH) (LOOHS) (KOH-LOH-RAH-DAH).
You failed to signal.	Usted no uso la señal.	(OOHS-TEHD) (NOH) (OOH-SOH) (LAH) (SEH-NYAHL).
You did not turn properly.	Usted no volteo correctamente.	(OOHS-TEHD) (NOH) (VOHL-TYOH) (KOH-REHK-TAH-MEHN-TEH).
Your lights were not working.	Sus luces no estaban trabajando.	(SOOHS) (LOOH-SEHS) (NOH) (EHS-TAH-BAHN) (TRAH-BAH-HAHN-DOH).
Your plates are expired.	Sus placas son vencidas.	(SOOHS) (PLAH-KAHS) (SOHN) (VEHN-SIH-DAHS).

Phrases

— TRAFFIC STOPS

English	Spanish	Pronounced
Your inspection sticker is expired.	Su etiqueta es vencida.	(SOOH) (EH-TIH-KEH-TAH) (EHS) (VEHN-SIH-DAH).
Who is the owner?	¿Quien es el dueño?	¿(KIH-YEHN) (EHS) (EHL) (DWEH-NYOH)?
Sign the ticket, please.	Firme la infraccion, por favor	(FIHR-MEH) (LAH) (IHN-FRAHK-SYOHN,) (POHR) (FAH-VOHR).
Your signature is your promise to appear in court on this date.	Su firme es su promesa de presentarse en corte esta fecha.	(SOOH) (FIHR-MAH) (EHS) (SOOH) (PROH-MEH-SAH) (DEH) (PREH-SEHN-TAHR-SEH) (EHN) (KOHR-TEH) (EHS-TAH) (FEH-CHAH).
Read the back, please, if you have questions.	Lea la reversa, por favor, si tiene preguntas.	(LEH-YAH) (LAH) (REH-VEHR-SAH,) (POHR) (FAH-VOHR,) (SIH) (TIH-YEH-NEH) (PREH-GOOHN-TAHS).

WITNESSES ———

English	Spanish	Pronounced
Who saw what happened?	¿Quien vio lo que paso?	¿(KIH-YEHN) (VIH-YOH) (LOH) (KEH) (PAH-SOH)?
When did it happen?	¿Cuando paso?	¿(KWAHN-DOH) (PAH-SOH)?
How many were there?	¿Cuantos eran?	¿(KWAHN-TOHS) (EH-RAHN)?
Do you know him?	¿Lo conoce?	¿(LOH) (KOH-NOH-SEH)?
What is his name?	¿Como se llama?	¿(KOH-MOH) (SEH) (YAH-MAH)?
Is he male or female?	¿Es hombre o mujer?	¿(EHS) (OHM-BREH) (O) (MOOH-HEHR)?
How tall?	¿Que tan alto?	¿(KEH) (TAHN) (AHL-TOH)?
How much did he weigh?	¿Cuanto pesa?	¿(KWAHN-TOH) (PEH-SAH)?
How old?	¿De que edad?	¿(DEH) (KEH) (EH-DAHD)?
Color of hair?	¿Color del pelo?	¿(KOH-LOHR) (DEHL) (PEH-LOH)?

Phrases

English	Spanish	Pronounced
Color of eyes?	¿Color de ojos?	¿(KOH-LOHR) (DEH) (OH-HOHS)?
Color of skin?	¿Color de su piel?	¿(KOH-LOHR) (DEH) (SOOH) (PIH-YEHL)?
Anglo?	¿Anglo?	¿(AHN-GLOH)?
Black?	¿Negro?	¿(NEH-GROH)?
Hispanic?	¿Hispano	¿(IHS-PAH-NOH)?
Oriental?	¿Oriental?	¿(OH-RIH-YEHN-TAHL)?
Color of clothing?	¿Color de ropa?	¿(KOH-LOHR) (DEH) (ROH-PAH)?
What color of cap?	¿De que color es la cachucha?	¿(DEH) (KEH) (KOH-LOHR) (EHS) (LAH) (KAH-CHOOH-CHAH)?
What color of shirt?	¿De que color es la camisa?	¿(DEH) (KEH) (KOH-LOHR) (EHS) (LAH) (KAH-MIH-SAH)?
What color of pants?	¿De que color son los pantalones?	¿(DEH) (KEH) (KOH-LOHR) (SOHN) (LOHS) (PAHN-TAH-LOH-NEHS)?
What color of dress?	¿De que color es el vestido?	¿(DEH) (KEH) (KOH-LOHR) (EHS) (EHL) (VEHS-TIH-DOH)?

WITNESSES ——

English	Spanish	Pronounced
What color of jacket?	¿De que color es el saco?	¿(DEH) (KEH) (KOH-LOHR) (EHS) (EHL) (SAH-KOH)?
What color of shoes?	¿De que color son los zapatos?	¿(DEH) (KEH) (KOH-LOHR) (SOHN) (LOHS) (ZAH-PAH-TOHS)?
What color of boots?	¿De que color son las botas?	¿(DEH) (KEH) (KOH-LOHR) (SOHN) (LAHS) (BOH-TAHS)
What color of beard?	¿De que color es la barba?	¿(DEH) (KEH) (KOH-LOHR) (EHS) (LAH) (BAHR-BAH)
What color of mustache?	¿De que color es el bigote?	¿(DEH) (KEH) (KOH-LOHR) (EHS) (EHL) (BIH-GOH-TEH)?
Does he/she have long hair?	¿Tiene pelo largo?	¿(TIH-YEN-NEH) (PEH-LOH) (LAHR-GOH)?
Does he/she have earrings?	¿Tiene aretes?	¿(TIH-YEN-NEH) (AH-REH-TEHS)?
What kind of motorcycle?	¿Que clase de motocicleta?	¿(KEH) (KLAHS-SEH) (DEH) (MOH-TOH-SIH-KLEH-TAH)?
What color?	¿Que color?	¿(KEH) (KOH-LOHR)?
Old or new?	¿Viejo o nuevo?	¿(VIH-YEH-HOH) (OH) (NWEH-VOH)?

— Witnesses

English	Spanish	Pronounced
Do you have the plate number?	¿Tiene el numero de la placa?	¿(TIH-YEH-NEH) (EHL) (NOOH-MEH-ROH) (DEH) (LAH) (PLAH-KAH)?
Which direction did they go in?	¿En que rumbo se fueron?	¿(EHN) (KEH) (RROOHM-BOH) (SEH) (FWEH-ROHN)?
Were they armed?	¿Estaban armados?	¿(EHS-TAH-BAHN) (AHR-MAH-DOHS)?
What is your name, sir?	¿Como se llama, usted?	¿(KOH-MOH) (SEH) (YAH-MAH,) (ÓOHS-TEHD)?
Your date of birth?	¿Su fecha de nacimiento?	¿(SOOH) (FEH-CHAH) (DEH) (NAH-SIH-MYEHN-TOH)?
Does he/she have tatoos?	¿Tiene tatuajes?	¿(TIH-YEH-NEH) (TAH-TWAH-HEHS)?
Does he/she have scars?	¿Tiene cicatriz?	¿(TIH-YEH-NEH) (SIH-KAH-TRIHS)?
Did he/she escape in a car or by foot?	¿Se escapo en carro o a pie?	¿(SEH) (EHS-KAH-POH) (EHN) (KAH-RROH) (OH) (AH) (PIH-YEH)?
What kind of car/truck?	¿Que clase de carro/troca?	¿(KEH) (KLAH-SEH) (DEH) (KAH-RROH/TROH-KAH)?

CHAPTER 4

Miranda Rights Warning

Miranda Rights Warning

Before asking you any questions, I would like you to recognize your rights.

1. You can remain silent. You are not obligated to make any statement, oral or written.

2. Any statement you make can be used against you in a court of law.

3. You have the right to speak with an attorney before speaking with us, and you have the right to have an attorney present during our questioning.

4. If you cannot afford an attorney, one will be appointed to represent you without cost to you.

5. You can speak with us without having an attorney, and you can stop talking at any time you like.

6. Your rights are continuous and can be urged by you at any time.
   Do you understand your rights?

Aviso de Sus Derechos

Antes de hacerle cualquier pregunta, quiero que usted reconosca sus derechos.

(AHN-TEHS) (DEH) (AH-SEHR-LEH) (KWAHL-KIH-YEHR) (PREH-GOOHN-TAH), (KIH-YEH-ROH) (KEH) (OOHS-TEHD) (REH-KOH-NOHS-KAH) (SOOHS) (DEH-REH-CHOS).

153

1. Usted puede guardar silencio. No esta obligado a declarar nada, oral o por escrito.

1. (OOHS-TEHD) (PWEH-DEH) (WAHR-DAHR) (SIH-LEHN-SYOH). (NOH) (EHS-TAHD) (OHB-LIH-GAH-DOH) (AH) (DEH-KLAH-RAHR) (NAH-DAH), (OH-RAHL) (OH) (POHR) (EHS-KRIH-TOH).

2. Lo que usted declare puede ser usado, en su contra, en una corte de ley.

2. (LOH) (KEH) (OOHS-TEHD) (DEH-KLAH-REH) (PWEH-DEH) (SEHR) (OOH-SAH-DOH), (EHN) (SOOH) (KOHN-TRAH), (EHN) (OOH-NAH) (KOHR-TEH) (DEH) (LAY).

3. Tiene el derecho de hablar con un abogado antes de hablar con nosotros y tiene el derecho de tener el abogado presente durante nuestras preguntas.

3. (TIH-YEH-NEH) (EHL) (DEH-REH-CHOH) (DEH) (AH-BLAHR) (KOHN) (OOHN) (AH-BOH-GAH-DOH) (AHN-TEHS) (DEH) (AH-BLAHR) (KOHN) (NOH-SOH-TROHS) (EE) (TIH-YEH-NEH) (EHL) (DEH-REH-CHOH) (DEH) (TEH-NEHR) (EHL) (AH-BOH-GAH-DOH) (PREH-SEHN-TEH) (DOOH-RAHN-TEH) (NWEHS-TRAHS) (PREH-GOOHN-TAHS).

4. Si usted no tiene el dinero para emplear un abogado, uno sera fijado para que lo represente, sin costo a usted.

4. (SIH) (OOHS-TEHD) (NOH) (TIH-YEH-NEH) (EHL) (DIH-NEH-ROH) (PAH-RAH) (EHM-PLEH-YAHR) (OOHN) (AH-BOH-GAH-DOH), (OOH-NOH) (SEH-RAH) (FIH-HAH-DOH) (PAH-RAH) (KEH) (LOH) (REH-PREH-SEHN-TEH), (SIHN) (KOHS-TOH) (AH) (OOHS-TEHD).

154

5. Usted puede hablar con nosotros sin tener un abogado presente y puede terminar su declaracion cuando usted quiera.

5. (OOHS-TEHD) (PWEH-DEH) (AH-BLAHR) (KOHN) (NOH-SOH-TROHS) (SIHN) (TEH-NEHR) (OOHN) (AH-BOH-GAH-DOH) (PREH-SEHN-TEH) (EE) (PWEH-DEH) (TEHR-MIH-NAHR) (SOOH) (DEH-KLAH-RAH-SYOHN) (KWAHN-DOH) (OOHS-TEHD) (KIH-YEH-RAH).

6. Sus derechos son continuos y pueden ser urgidos a cualquier tiempo.

6. (SOOHS) (DEH-REH-CHOHS) (SOHN) (KOHN-TIH-NOOH-OHS), (EE) (PWEH-DEHN) (SEHR) (OOHR-HEEH-DOHS) (AH) (KWAHL-KIH-YEHR) (TIH-YEHM-POH).

¿Comprendio sus derechos?
(KOHM-PREHN-DIH-YOH) (SOOHS) (DEH-REH-CHOHS)

INDEX

ENGLISH & SPANISH CROSS-REFERENCES

A

161

I

173

175

R

ENGLISH PHRASE INDEX

SPANISH WORD INDEX

197

204

SPANISH PHRASE INDEX

231

— NOTES —

— NOTES —

— NOTES —

— NOTES —

— NOTES —

— NOTES —

— NOTES —